# CITY OF KASHMIR

SAMEER HAMDANI

# City of Kashmir
*Srinagar, A Popular History*

HURST & COMPANY, LONDON

First published in the United Kingdom in 2025 by
C. Hurst & Co. (Publishers) Ltd.,
New Wing, Somerset House, Strand, London, WC2R 1LA
© Sameer Hamdani, 2025
All rights reserved.

Distributed in the United States, Canada and Latin America by Oxford University Press, 198 Madison Avenue, New York, NY 10016, United States of America.

The right of Sameer Hamdani to be identified as the author of this publication is asserted by him in accordance with the Copyright, Designs and Patents Act, 1988.

A Cataloguing-in-Publication data record for this book is available from the British Library.

ISBN: 9781911723769

EU GPSR Authorised Representative
Easy Access System Europe Oü, 16879218
Address: Mustamäe tee 50, 10621, Tallinn, Estonia
Contact Details: gpsr.requests@easproject.com, +358 40 500 3575

Printed and bound in Great Britain by Bell and Bain Ltd, Glasgow

www.hurstpublishers.com

*To an ancestor, Mulla Sa'id al-Din Hamdani,
who made it to Srinagar, many centuries back*

The past, is it of any consequence?
Which bits to remember, and which to forget?
And who owns the past?

# CONTENTS

*Acknowledgements* — xi
*Note on Dates and* Translation — xiii

Introduction — 1

## I
## CITY IN THE TEXT

1. Prelude — 7
2. The One Who Conquered All — 19
3. The City of Pravara — 31
4. Mongols and Turks — 55
5. Shahr-i Kashmir — 65
6. Khanqah-i Maula — 71
7. Nau Shahr — 83
8. Jamia-i Srinagar — 89
9. Dumath — 97
10. A Mughal Emperor in the City — 103

| 11. | Mazar-i Shoura | 117 |
| 12. | Raghunath Mandir | 125 |
| 13. | The Bund | 131 |
| 14. | City on a Map | 139 |

## II
## CITY AND LIFE

| 15. | An Assembly of Poets | 149 |
| 16. | Saint of the City | 157 |
| 17. | The Bagh (Garden) | 163 |
| 18. | Saeer (Outing) | 177 |
| 19. | Chiragan (Illumination) | 185 |
| 20. | Chai | 195 |
| 21. | An Iranian Lady in the City | 203 |
| 22. | Tanz-o Mizah (Satire) | 211 |
| 23. | Nar (Fire) | 215 |
| 24. | Tajiran-i Shahr | 219 |
| 25. | A City in Revolt | 227 |

| *Notes* | 235 |
| *Bibliography* | 245 |
| *Index* | 249 |

# ACKNOWLEDGEMENTS

THIS IS A BOOK that changed its shape as I wrote it: the process of writing did, at times, challenge my desire to continue with the project. I wish to thank all my friends who encouraged me to finish: Umer Farooq, Mujtaba Qadri, Mehran Qureshi, Mehmood Shah, Rauf Shaw, Pirzada Ashiq, and Taha Mughal. Mehran needs a special mention for the translations he was kind enough to provide for some of the Persian verses I have used in this book. I look forward to the day when he publishes his compilation.

I am thankful to Faizaan Bhat, Shakir Mir and Haroon Rashid for sharing numerous valuable books from their libraries and for letting them remain with me. I did return them in the end, though, after a prolonged delay. Thanks to Tabish Ghazi for making available many of the images that became part of my research.

I am indebted to several individuals who shared their stories and memories about the city: Saleem Beg, Zahid G Muhammad, Siddiq Wahid, Ghulam Muhammad Guroo, Munshi Rafiq, Anubhuti Maurya, Sumaira Hakak, Ifthikhar Hakim, Munshi Iftikhar, Tahmina Riyaz, Imran Ali Buth, Shoaib Qasba, Sheikh Muhammad Shafi, Samir Turki, Enus Khan, Imdad Saqi, Nazir

# ACKNOWLEDGEMENTS

Masoodi, Naseer Ganai, Muhammad Yasin Zuhra, Basit Abu Bakr, Sayyid Zafar Safvi and Munshi Ashraf.

I am very grateful to Ebba Koch and Wheeler Thackston for sharing their thoughts on the nature of Mughal engagement in Kashmir. Thanks to MH Zafar, Luther Oberock and Mrinal Koul for their valuable insights into the Sanskrit world of medieval Kashmir; and to Amanda Lanzillo for introducing me to native writings on manufacturing in India during the colonial period. I am also thankful to Yale Rice for sharing a nineteenth-century album at Amherst College, which provides an interesting perspective on life in Kashmir.

I owe thanks to the National Archives, Delhi; the Metropolitan Museum, New York; and the British Library, London, all of whose online resources have been crucial to my research work. I owe special gratitude to Zoya Khan for reproducing the historical maps I have used in this book; and to Basita Shah for being kind enough to share two of her paintings.

I would also like to thank the wonderful staff at the Oriental Research Library and the SPS Museum, Srinagar, who have always been welcoming and helpful during my research.

To my literary agent, Kanishka Gupta, for persevering with me despite the delays in finishing this manuscript. The same goes for my publishers, for their endless patience.

To my parents, Shaukat Ali and Bismillah Rizvi, special thanks for encouraging my interest in the past when many believe it to be a futile exercise. I owe a big debt to my mother for all those amazing stories about people, families and the city she has shared with me. Some, I hope, will make their way into a future story. To my daughter, Parirou, I express the hope that you may never be indifferent to your past and your history. And, to my wife, Rakshanda, special thanks!

# NOTES ON DATES AND TRANSLATION

ALL DATES IN THE text are from the Common Era (CE), unless otherwise indicated. I have mostly followed popular Kashmiri renditions of proper names as well as place names. So Parihaspur rather than Parihasporā. Similarly, I have used the more popular Kashmiri name, Khanqah-i Maula and not the original Persian, Khānqāh-i Mʿaulā. I have also avoided the use of diacritical markings to make the text more accessible for general readership.

# INTRODUCTION

FOR MANY OF ITS inhabitants, the city of Srinagar exists as a memory of what it was, and not what it is. On social media, any post depicting old images of the city—with its maze of streets, shops and lanes; and underpaid, overworked artisans working in dimly lit *karkhanas* (workshops)—generates an immediate and often overwhelming response. Often, the same set of images, in both black and white and colour, which had captured the imagination of European visitors to the region in the nineteenth and twentieth centuries, is recycled year after year, in an endless loop of rediscovery of the cityscape, now mostly lost. Even poverty, which was endemic to the city till the second half of the last century, is celebrated; after all, it highlights the *syezar ti pazar*, the simplicity and truthfulness of our ancestors. Colourless, grainy images also serve as a perfect medium to bring into focus the simplicity of past lives. Within the grim, dull greyness that defines contemporary Srinagar, the past somewhat paradoxically adds a certain richness, both real and, at times, imagined. People connect, they respond, and a narrative of linked memories unfolds. *Those were pious times, simple times, and the best of times!* The past, idyllic and picturesque, stands in stark contrast to today's troubled and fractured reality. But, then, should anyone be surprised with such a reaction, given the city's recent history?

Memories, after all, are evocative; they can be easily romanticized. And we seldom pick a quarrel with them. Instead, we frame and arrange memories into impressive, neat and contained collages, showcasing past greatness or else present-day betrayal. Like a make-believe city, these carefully curated bits of images, tales and realities can serve as an alternative to the actual pulse of a living city: the sweaty and often grim, but mostly loud and spirited, throbbing, screeching cry of life that is a city. It was in the lanes of the city that our elders once cried out: "The present in a city is never utopian unless you are a Sufi!"

So how does one write the history of a city that claims an existence of a few millennia? It's a bit difficult, given the rich literary and oral traditions that locate the city at the intersection of three major faiths, Buddhism, Hinduism and Islam. The intellectual and cultural experiences that informed the artistic traditions governing the visuals of cityscapes owed much to the courts of great empires located within the plains of South Asia: the Kushans, the Huns, the Guptas and the Mughals. But the city has also inherited one enduring and grim legacy from the past: the Partition. The conflict between India and Pakistan defines both the present and future for all Kashmiris. With both nations heavily invested in Kashmir's future, Srinagar's fortunes periodically oscillate from hope to despair, and back again.

This book, the first of a two-volume work, is my first venture into popular history. It is located at the intersection of the city's urban history, crafts, politics, religions and trade—but is also tempered with a degree of memory—glimpses of past days, some personal, some inherited. For those who have wandered through the alluring physical landscape of the city, its lakes and waterways; walked the *kochas* (narrow lanes) of the ancient-looking *mohallas* (neighbourhoods); and felt the power of the city's numerous

## INTRODUCTION

shrines and *khanqahs* (Sufi hospices), the canvas this book offers may be too small. As a friend once told me, life always finds a way to grow in the interstices; so even if my story falls woefully short, this is not the end of the saga that is Srinagar.

# I

# CITY IN THE TEXT

# 1

PRELUDE

> *In your love, I lost my night, my day*
> *In the hope of your love, I lost my night, my day*
> *Come, my beloved, to you I sing.*
>
> Nyami Saeeb (1805–1865),
> Sufi poet from Srinagar

IT WAS THE GREAT Indian columnist, the late Kuldip Nayar, who once said that life in an Indian city is like living in a bazaar.[1] Anyone who has travelled to a city not only in India but across major parts of South Asia will readily agree. Amidst all the colours and flavours, there is an inherent loudness, a boisterousness and a certain cacophony of sounds that lend a chaotic vibrancy to city life in India. But not so in Srinagar, or at least not in the historic parts of the city. Even in its most lively and celebratory mood, Srinagar tends to be inward-looking and reflective; maybe argumentative but never disruptively loud.

Cities in South Asia are old; only a few can be termed modern. Some, like the holy Hindu city of Banaras, are truly ancient. The pulsating heart of a living faith, Banaras is what you desire it to be. In the 1960s and 1970s, the city became part of the Hippie Trail, a destination for those disillusioned with life in the West, wandering in search of *nirvana*. Today, Banaras stands reincarnated as the symbol of a resurgent far-right Hindu politics, erasing anything that stands in its way. Then there are imperial Muslim cities such as Delhi, Agra and Lahore, which seem more medieval, though the sites they occupy are nearly as ancient as Banaras itself. Even in decay, as they fade away, a whiff of past glory remains. But for how long? We also have planned cities, like Chandigarh, a city that just emerged from empty fields in the 1950s to provide shelter to countless thousands rendered homeless by the Partition. Chandigarh remains a favourite with architecture students, amazed by the sheer vitality of a newly established republic and its utopian quest for providing its citizens with the comforts of modern life. Some, like me, find the Corbusian architecture about which the city boasts a bit whimsical and trite but would rarely voice such heresies in public—apart from during college days. In the 1990s, when I was studying in an architecture school in Delhi, a senior once remarked that Chandigarh was a permanent reminder of the brilliance and the hubris of its French architect. This certainly did not go down well with the teachers for whom Le Corbusier was an icon. I myself still agree with the sentiment.

In the streets and alleys of its old quarters—the *mohallas* of the downtown area—Srinagar, the "city of Sri" or the Hindu goddess of wealth, Lakshmi,[2] displays the charm of respectability, not as ancient as Banaras but still of a respectable age, older than Delhi or Lahore. And in written texts, the city boasts an even more ancient and venerable ancestry, its mythical past dating back a couple of millennia. Yet increasingly, this "charm"—the texture of the old Srinagar—is being lost. New neighbourhoods that have emerged on reclaimed marshes, paddy lands or orchards threaten to suffocate the historical city with their ugliness and lack of identity. Their generic appearance and imported aesthetics are antithetical to the historic Srinagar. The old and the new are perpetually colliding: the new seeks to obliterate traces of the old, while the old lies imprisoned in the past, simply unable to cope with life. Rarely do the two intersect or combine into something meaningful. Sometimes the present does seek to fuse with the past, but the final "product" always tends to be kitschy: popular, sometimes even decently picturesque, but contextually flawed. There is never a fusion that works magisterially.

# PRELUDE

As an urban mass, Srinagar occupies an envious position; it is located almost in the middle of a physical landscape, simultaneously powerful and mesmerizing. The city lies in the heart of the Kashmir valley—this is how the tourist guides explain it to visitors. For a tourist whose experience of the city is limited to a night's stay, the view from the balcony of a hotel room on the Boulevard, overlooking the Dal Lake, can be quite tempting if you are in the mood to be tempted. Srinagar appears as one large verdant landscape framed by mountains and filled with expansive lake waters that reflect the flickering night lights from the numerous wooden houseboats marooned on their surface. The visual tropes commonly found in visitor information align perfectly. Srinagar is advertised as a paradise—*jannat*—and so it seems. Its landscape has, in the past, moved emperors, kings, poets and visitors into moments of pure ecstasy and wonderment. Even in the older sections of the city, the more you delve into its narrow, winding streets, the more extraordinary it seems. There is always a surprise and a visual spectacle hidden somewhere.

But the exoticized Kashmir and, by extension, the equally fetishized Srinagar occupy a narrative that soon becomes simply repetitive, devoid of any meaning, at times even puerile. However, the story of Kashmir as a paradisical land is not limited to visitors alone. Growing up in Kashmir, at a certain moment of life, you get sold on the idea of viewing your surroundings as *jannat*. You are told about the beauty of the land, about its uniqueness. Kashmir is the terrestrial paradise, and Srinagar is the city of this paradise. Often this popular perception is also marked by a genuine notion of its matchless incomparability. But then, as a people, Kashmiris tend to have a wonderful belief in their abilities and the uniqueness of their land.

Historically, for the people of Kashmir, Srinagar is the only city in their land. There are innumerable villages, and there are many historical towns, but there is only one single *shahr*—the city of Srinagar. To be an inhabitant of the *shahr* brings with it all the privileges, comforts and biases that a sedentary urban life bestows. The city suggests it is all-knowing; like an *aagur* (the source of a spring), the fountainhead of knowledge; and it parades its sophistication. It is the marker of culture as well as of cultural spaces, and also the mannerisms that define culture—*adab*. Even in medieval times, the city was seen as a seat of culture, designed to impress, and quite distinct from the rural landscape, which was portrayed not only as inherently rustic but also as something primitive and rather simple. The Sanskrit poet Kshemendra (d. 1070), who studied under the greatest aesthete Kashmir ever produced, Abhinavagupta (c. 975–1025), decried those unversed in the subtleties of his craft as "newly arrived, overawed bumpkin[s] in the depths of the big city".[3]

Kshemendra was a prolific writer whose plays, with their biting satire, seem to be specially designed to present medieval Kashmiri society as a culturally and socially morbid space. But his remark is also a commemoration of the poet's roots, located as they are in an urbane courtly circle. What Kshemendra suggests gradually insinuated itself into the mood of the city, so that the inhabitants of Srinagar came to believe that the only *suhbat* (company) that deserved to be cultivated was the city. In the nineteenth century, a poet from Srinagar, Mulla Hakim Habib-al Lah (1852–1904), who mainly wrote religious elegies, composed his *Greist Nama* (Book of Village Life), a not-so-polite satire on why to avoid the *suhbat* of someone from outside the *shahr*. This work, which would certainly offend modern sensibilities, starts on a note of imparting *nasihat* (counsel):

> Hearken to my counsel, count the ills that are there,
> Should you take to companionship, someone from a village
> Their souls are different: this one from the city, and the other from a village,

## PRELUDE

> Never will the two be bound together: one sweet, the other bitter and venomous[4]

Habib's imagery is filled with the dominant tropes of nineteenth-century urban life that seek to belittle those from outside the city because of their mannerisms. In another, earlier work of the same name, we see a more extreme dehumanization of rural existence. In a lengthy *masnavi*,[5] Pir Maqbool Shah Kralwari (1820–1877) depicted the villager as someone devoid of humanity: immoral, irreligious, animal-like. Surprisingly, the composer of this older *Greist Nama* was himself a villager. Seen as one of the leading Kashmiri lyricists of the nineteenth century, Kralwari, like Habib, hailed from an upper-class Muslim background. But while Habib's misgivings are essentially reductive, with the spatial geography of the city serving as the marker of class and culture, Kralwari seeks to position himself as urbane, defined by interlinked bloodlines that connect him to the city culture despite being a non-resident. As someone from the upper class, Kralwari's social positioning sets him apart from his peers in the village, identifying him as their superior. Essentially, the *suhbat* that both Habib and Kralwari promote is both discriminatory and exclusive. Often in the past as well as today, this exclusiveness remains the mood, the *mizaj*, of the city. Yet, notwithstanding discrimination, the city continues to draw in people who make it their home. And, in a generation or two, the newcomers adopt the mannerisms of the city, they become people of the city, their roots hidden if not entirely forgotten.

But then there is another side to Srinagar. It is also a city that thrives on and promotes cultural and social synthesis and sustains a vibrant community life; a city that is still rooted in cross-culturalism despite the losses of recent decades, which saw the unravelling of the city's social fabric. The architecture, crafts, cuisine, clothing—the aesthetics of city life—are clear examples of the cultural hybridity that stands at the heart of the city's culture. A deeper examination lifts the veil to reveal how diverse cultures from the Indian plains, as well as from regions as diverse as the Tibetan highlands, Central Asia, and, even further afield, the Roman and the Hellenic world, have left their marks on the everyday life of the city in a seemingly unique way. This process of exchange, which could be experienced on the streets and the river of Srinagar till very recent times, was only interrupted by the emergence of the modern nation-states of India and Pakistan. One may wonder at this incongruous independence, which resulted in a disruption of the ways people and cultures had interacted for generations.

A few years back, an online acquaintance mailed me an image of what looked like an official document. It was a family possession, but the owners, an old merchant family of Srinagar, were unfamiliar with its content—and were curious. The document was bilingual, in an illegible Persian scribal script, *shikasta*, and what seemed like Tibetan. All I could decipher was the date 1218 AH (1803 CE), a few names, and a reference to a continuing privilege of access. The document bore multiple seals, one of which, in faded red, looked very official. So I shared the image with someone familiar with the Tibetan world, Siddiq Wahid, an academic with a wide interest in cultural linkages and networks connecting Kashmir, Ladakh, Tibet and the wider Central Asia. It turned out that the document was an official permit giving access to Tibet, a much-frequented place for Kashmiri merchants and traders, especially those engaged in the pashmina trade. The seal was that of the Dalai Lama.

Not so long ago, on 31 July 1823, William Moorcroft (d. 1825), an English explorer and a spy in the services of the East India Company, left Srinagar to visit the city of Bukhara in present-day Uzbekistan. The journey took place in the shadow of the Great Game, the battle for supremacy in Central Asia

PRELUDE

between Russia and the British Empire, and it would, in the end, cost Moorcroft his life. Yet on the day of his departure, Srinagar must have presented a sunny, colourful spectacle as the English explorer embarked on his boat with an entourage which, in his own words, resembled "the greatest variety of nations that ever marched together, enrolling English, Hindustanis, Gorkhas, Tibetans, Persians, Kashmiris, Kurds and Turks, in its ranks".[6]

While most of these ventures were mercantile and resulted in the production, trafficking and consumption of high-value products and luxury items, sometimes the mercantile exchanges also resulted in unique and unintended outcomes of cross-culturalism. The Oriental Library in Srinagar houses the largest collection of manuscripts produced in Kashmir and includes works in Arabic, Hindi, Kashmiri, Persian and Sanskrit. Despite its name, a leftover from the colonial past, the library is a cultural treasure trove for those who love manuscripts. Many of the manuscripts, especially those in Sanskrit, were collected in the second half of the rule of the Dogra dynasty (1846–1947), highlighting the cultural proclivities of a court invested in the promotion of the Hindu faith and learning. This was followed by numerous new acquisitions in the years between the 1950s and 1970s, from family libraries spread across Kashmir but mostly centred on Srinagar. Given the cultural mood of the city, most of this new collection featured work composed in Persian, a language that had served the court and the city elite for the previous six centuries.

The collection also includes several independent folios of Persian and Arabic calligraphy dating to the nineteenth century. Under the Mughals, the art of making imperial albums (*muraqqa nigari*) was a much-valued art form. The Mughal album is an exquisite assemblage of calligraphy and painting with an equally intricate border pasted and joined together. The art historian Ebba Koch describes *muraqqa* as a "book in form and a picture gallery in function".[7] The art was widely favoured in Srinagar, and during the eighteenth and nineteenth centuries the city emerged as a major centre for the production of finely executed calligraphic works. These included manuscripts of the Quran, the Mahabharata, Persian poetry, and a diverse range of religious and secular works. The Oriental Library collection also includes a set of more than a hundred variegated calligraphic works. A few are decorated with an interesting and uniquely nineteenth-century border composition: stamps of European companies, showing the influence of advancing colonialism on an art form that was perfected in South Asia under the Mughals. The collection further includes a folio which impresses with the vitality of Kashmir's past trans-regional links. On a sheet of paper which had originally served as an advertisement for a textile merchant—possibly a silk merchant in Suzhou, China[8]—a calligrapher in Srinagar penned verses from the *diwan* of the famous Persian poet Hafiz Shirazi (d. 1390). The manner in which this small folio of art came into existence, linking China, Persia and Kashmir—cultures which in the past shared a widespread connection—is unimaginable today.

Though life in Srinagar was privileged, the city's existence was also marked with pain, gloom, exploitation, suffering and death. From medieval times, the city remained the site of looting and oppression. Destiny seems to have marked it as a site of contestations and conquests. It was burned, rebuilt and burned again, repeatedly—conquered and humiliated into submission, despoiled of its wealth, mocked for its poverty. Even mercantile wealth, located in a native class of merchants and traders, the *khwajas*, and the source behind the construction and upkeep of much of the city's public architecture, was itself sourced from the labour and plight of a workforce living in abject poverty. Despite the well-meaning philanthropy of the merchants and traders, witnessed in times of civic distress, the commerce of the city was never based on an ethical functioning. It was, and continues to be, exploitative. The transgressions of the merchant class and the plight of their workforce, both Kashmiris, were sufficiently powerful to move the poet-philosopher Allama Iqbal (1877–1938) to write,

> The khwaja dressed in a fine robe, woven by your hands,
> And you, condemned to tatters, each thread laid bare.[9]

Yet, despite the odds, the city survived. And, while in the nineteenth century the city's ascendancy as the sole urban centre of Kashmir was unquestionable, historically there were times when even Srinagar's survival was threatened.

# 2

# THE ONE WHO CONQUERED ALL

> *basti basna khel nahin*
> *bastey bastey basti hey*
>
> For a settlement to prosper,
> is not a child's play
> incrementally,
> in bits and pieces,
> it settles and prospers.
>
> Fani Badayuni (d. 1941), Urdu poet

IN THE EIGHTH CENTURY, a Kashmiri king came to dominate the Indian plains from his Himalayan kingdom, breaking the physical isolation of his mountainous land. This brief, meteoric rise concerned a king whose name in Sanskrit signifies "the one whose diadem is taken off". Muktapida Lalitaditya (r. 724–760), the fourth ruler from the House of Karkota, belonged to a dynasty that would rule Kashmir from the seventh till the middle of the ninth century. The dynasty was established by Lalitaditya's father, Durlabhaka, also known as Pratapaditya.[1] In the verses of Kalhana, the twelfth-century Kashmiri poet and historian, the extent of Lalitaditya's conquests stretch across most of South Asia, touching the southernmost tip of this vast and diverse geography. Whether real or imagined, in the poet's narrative the Kashmiri army under Lalitaditya's command crossed over the Jhelum river (Vitasta, in Sanskrit), embarking on a world-conquering journey that saw them wading through the waters of Ganga and Caveri, and moving all the way down to the coast of

Malabar in South India. Given his exploits, Kalhana eulogized the king as Digvijaya, "the one who conquered all". To mark his victories, the king initiated a tradition of erecting triumphal monuments in the cities he had conquered. In the end, these monuments proved to be as ephemeral as his battle victories, as no trace of them still exists or has been excavated.

Much like Alexander before him, Lalitaditya would meet his end on a military campaign, one undertaken in or beyond the icy mountains of Karakoram. Before his end, the exhausted king would see his all-conquering army perish before his own eyes, the result of an ill-timed winter campaign in the north, somewhere beyond the Tibetan highlands. The exact location where the king and his army perished is uncertain. Rather typically, Kashmiri writers imagine his last moments taking place further afield, in more distant lands. In these legends, the warrior king's death occurred in the deserts of Central Asia, or maybe even Iran, at that time part of the Abbasid Caliphate (750–1258). It was not a mortal enemy but fate alone that defeated Lalitaditya.

Centuries later, when Kalhana was writing *Rajatarangini*, the only material evidence of Lalitaditya's triumphs was a series of war trophies—flags captured from kingdoms in the plains of South Asia—annually paraded in the streets of Srinagar, the capital of Kashmir. At a time when the political might of Kashmir was declining, this ceremonial passage through the city was but a feeble echo of a glorious past. Given the political turbulence of twelfth-century Kashmir, which operated as a political arena of contested authority, this annual cycle served no meaning. It remained a visual spectacle devoid of any political consequence.

For Kalhana, living in twelfth-century Kashmir, then unstable and rebellious, the exploits of Lalitaditya held the irresistible appeal of a hero. In his history, which at times is also used for a didactic purpose, the image of Lalitaditya stands largely unblemished. So it is not surprising that while Kalhana provides his audience with many details about Lalitaditya, he fails to account for the help that the Kashmiri king sought and received from the T'ang emperor of China Xuanzong (r. 712–756),[2] who ruled China for 44 years. Xuanzong would institute a forward defence policy to control incursions on his northern border from both the Tibetans and the Turks. This resulted in a military alliance with the king of Kashmir, in the context of Tibetan advances on Gilgit starting in 722. The territory of Gilgit-Baltistan,[3] which marked the northern boundary of Kashmir, had served as a Chinese tributary. This region also formed the land route for trade between Kashmir and China through the Tarim Basin and on to the Silk Road. Against a backdrop of military incursions, battles and peace treaties drawn up and then torn apart, hostilities between the Chinese and the Tibetans would continue to plague Xuanzong's reign. Lalitaditya's overtures to the Chinese benefited both against a common threat, the Tibetans. In return for military help, Lalitaditya acknowledged Chinese suzerainty: this is the account that is given in the T'ang chronicles.

Simultaneously, when Lalitaditya was engaged in his campaigns, a new dynasty, the Abbasid, would claim the Muslim caliphate and come to occupy much of Central Asia. Soon thereafter, in 751, the Abbasids defeated the T'ang army in a decisive battle at the Talas River, on the Silk Road near present-day Kyrgyzstan. This marked the beginning of T'ang withdrawal from Central Asia and, more importantly, that of Buddhism. With Central Asia gradually opening to Islam, repercussions would be felt in regions as far away as South Asia, including Kashmir. In such circumstances, it seems highly improbable that Lalitaditya did indeed march his armies further westward into Iran. But then it does raise an interesting possibility. What if the Kashmiri king also perished in the Battle of Talas? It seems likely that a Kashmiri contingent accompanied the Chinese in the battle. And the accounts that we have of the Chinese rout at Talas almost mirror the reports that have survived in Kashmir about Lalitaditya's death. But, then, accidental similarity is never the same as historical certainty.

Away from the glories and triumphs of distant battlefields, the loot and the plunder of conquest helped Lalitaditya set up a court that witnessed the efflorescence of a new, bold and distinct style, what we may retrospectively call the Kashmiri school. It was in this one big moment that Kashmir finally emerged from the shadows of more ancient traditions, those linked to Gandhara and Taxila, lands located to the west of Kashmir. To indicate this new beginning, the conqueror sought a rupture with the past. The epicentre of this creative spirit and new beginning was a new city, Parihaspur (modern Devar-Parihaspora), and not the historical Srinagar. With his new city, located on tableland fourteen miles northwest of Srinagar, the Kashmir of Lalitaditya was inaugurated.

Parihaspur is the site where Lalitaditya sought to stage his geopolitical fantasies as a triumphant king. Even today, on a clear spring day, the crumbling ruins of Parihaspur command a fine view of Srinagar, visually dominating this ancient, rival city. For the king, though, the image of a victor was provided by the most common architectural device, a monumental victory pillar. Located in front of his palace at Parihaspur, the pillar was adorned with royal banners and surmounted by a stone-carved image of Garuda, the mount of the Hindu deity Lord Vishnu. Comprising a single block of stone, 21 metres (54 cubits) in length, the pillar was probably the largest stone monolith in medieval India. The imagery of a symbol linked with the cult of Vishnu hovering magnificently above the new city manifested Lalitaditya's desire to promote Kashmir's appeal to a wider Indian audience as the "only great Hindu kingdom left standing".[4] This followed the vacuum that had been left by the demise of the Gupta Empire earlier, in the sixth century. Most scholars believe that it was under the Karkota that Kashmir transformed from a Buddhist to a Hindu land. Lalitaditya's father, Durlabhaka, is credited with making a conscious effort to cultivate a unique Hindu habitus in Kashmir, one grounded in the cult of Vishnu. Similarly, the Karkota kings supported the resettlement in Kashmir of Brahmins from the Gangetic plains. The commissioning of the *Visnudharmottara Purana*, a Sanskrit text favouring Vaishnavism, is also attributed to Durlabhaka. This work again highlights the desire of the Karkota dynasty to integrate Kashmir with the broader Indic civilization and mark the land with the cult of Vishnu, a cult predominant in the Indian plains, as opposed to Shaivism, which was popular in Kashmir. In line with this sectarian proclivity of the early Karkota kings, Lalitaditya also consecrated five magnificent temples to Vishnu at Parihaspur.

On Lalitaditya's death, the capital moved back to Srinagar, and gradually the city declined. Unfortunately, today at Parihaspur not much survives, aside from the stone plinths of three buildings long ago destroyed and vandalized. Much of the city was quarried by succeeding generations of rulers to build their own temples and monasteries. Some seven miles west of Parihaspur, at Pattan, King Shankaravarman (883–902), of the Utpala dynasty, consecrated the Sugandesha Temple. The temple bears the name of the king's wife, Queen Sugandha, who ruled Kashmir for a brief period following her husband's death. Generously restored in the twentieth century by the Archaeological Survey of India, the temple imitates established prototypes dating from Lalitaditya's time. The inner walls of the temple, though, resemble a mismatch of ill-fitting stones, highlighting their source from an older site: Parihaspur. This was to be the character of medieval architecture in Kashmir: vandalize, steal, and create.

Meanwhile, it was during his residence at Parihaspur that legends speak about how on one fateful night, from the balcony of his palace, Lalitaditya raged against Srinagar. From the high ground of Parihaspur, the king could still see the glittering lights of the former capital. They seemed to mock his ability to conquer, and the king must have realized his failure in relocating his subjects to the new capital. Srinagar, even if no longer the seat of power, continued to flourish, much to the annoyance of Lalitaditya. The inebriated king ordered the city to be burned. For Parihaspur to flourish, Srinagar had to perish.

Kalhana describes Srinagar as a city of towers, filled with a great number of mansions each soaring to a height of a hundred feet or more. Today the tallest house in the city would barely reach half that height. For Lalitaditya, Srinagar with its tall towers seemed to be mocking Parihaspur as a pretentious upstart. So, in a fit of drunken madness, he ordered the city to be burned. But the tragedy was averted by courtiers who, by burning torches in the darkness of the night, convinced the inebriated monarch that the old capital was indeed on fire. Much to his relief, the king found his old capital intact the next morning. Realizing the enormity of his act, the mortified king issued a new decree: orders issued under the influence of spirits could be safely ignored. This is how Kalhana reports the event.

Srinagar had survived, and the king let it be. While Lalitaditya continued to favour Parihaspur, Srinagar also remained a vibrant *polis*. The city was still filled with wealth despite the emergence of Parihaspur. When the ancestors of the sage Abhinavagupta relocated to Kashmir from Kannuj in the Gangetic plains, Lalitaditya rewarded them with a mansion in Srinagar, located on the Jhelum. In *Tantralouk*, his magnum opus on philosophy and tantric ritualism, Abhinavagupta briefly speaks about the migration of an ancestor, Artigupta, and his taking up residence in Srinagar: "In that city on the bank of Vitasta, the king had created the dwelling of Artigupta facing the temple of Siva who used to move in the city of Kubera, the god of wealth."⁵

Abhinavagupta was a resident of Srinagar and spent the greater part of his life living and teaching there. His work is still seen as a fundamental text for understanding the Shivite school associated with Kashmiri Hindusim as well as for appreciating Indian aesthetics. Though we fail to get a glimpse of contemporary social life or the urban landscape in his writings, Abhinavagupta does briefly touch upon the city, including a description of a magnificent Shiv temple consecrated by Pravarasena at Pravarapur. The philosopher was a lifelong celibate and also a practising tantric who elaborated in *Tantralouk* on ritualistic sex as the means of acquiring supreme bliss. For Abhinava, sex, wine and women combine to create the same feeling as psychedelic drugs in modern society-enhanced sensory perceptions. In *Daksinamurti*, a text possibly authored by a student of Abhinavagupta, we find the teacher seated in the middle of his garden, embodying the presiding deity of a profound spiritual moment, *ananda*, or supreme spiritual bliss. Modern sensibilities, however, might interpret this as an exemplar of hedonistic existence. If the text is not seen as an example of rhetorical exaggeration, then it does capture the aesthetics particular to and prevalent in the medieval cosmopolis that was Srinagar:

> In the middle of a garden of grapes, inside a pavilion made of crystal and filled with beautiful paintings. The room smells wonderful because of flower garlands, incense sticks and (oil-)lamps. Its wall is smeared with sandal-paste [...] resounding with musical instruments, with songs and with dancing. There are crowds of women Yogins [...] to his side two women, partners in Tantric rites (*duti*), who hold in one hand a jug of wine (*sivarasa*) and a box of betel rolls, and in other hand a lotus and citron. Abhinava has his eyes

trembling in ecstasy [...] he plays on his resonating lute with
the tips of the quivering fingers of his lotus-like left hand.⁶

The text definitively captures a mood, a deeply sensuous moment.
But aside from that, it also provides evidence of a tradition of
garden keeping in the city. In the seventeenth century, after
conquering Kashmir, the Mughals would embellish the land as
a terrestrial paradise—*jannat firdous*, or simply the Bagh (the
Garden). The pavilion would be transformed into a lofty *baradari*,
having much in common with the wooden pillared porticos and
halls found in Safavid Iran. At the time of Abhinavagupta, aside
from private gardens, the city boasted public gardens, one which
is named by Kalhana as Rajana.

Years later, Abhinavagupta would leave the city for the
seclusion of the countryside, where he would contemplate and
practise his philosophy. Towards the end, he is rumoured to have
entered a cave with twelve hundred disciples, never to return. His
works would continue to inspire many in the city, acting as the
keepers of the city's aesthetic mood.

Parihaspur's glory proved short-lived. Till very recent times,
the site served as an open source for quarrying large blocks of
limestone. The abundance of stones on the plateau of Parihaspur
also gave this once royal city the name by which ordinary
Kashmiris still remember it: Kani Shahr (The Stone City).
Somewhere in the 1990s, a senior minister in the government
of Kashmir is said to have toyed with the idea of re-establishing
Parihaspur as the state capital. As opposed to what was perceived
as the organic mess of Srinagar, the new capital was to be a
modern city, with clean, broad avenues, well-provided services,
and the planned demarcation of residential and administrative
areas. The obsession with straight, wide roads is something that
politicians, bureaucrats and planners seem unable to get over.
How the banal uniformity that epitomizes modern cities can

inspire, or enhance the rich visuals of a historic city, remains an unexplained mystery. Though at times the old city of Srinagar feels like a forgotten community, the proposal created enough public backlash for the idea to be stillborn, quickly buried and forgotten. Srinagar outlived both a feudal ruler and an elected minister.

# 3

# THE CITY OF PRAVARA

THE SITE OF PRAVARAPUR, or, as it is often referred to in medieval Sanskrit texts, the City of Pravara, marks the beginning of historical Srinagar. It represents a complex layer of mixed identities, located at the formation of Kashmiri culture and its history. It also highlights how the foundation of this Kashmiri city borrowed from a range of diverse regions, cultures and ethnicities both from the Gangetic plains in the south and from lands to the west and north of Kashmir.

In medieval Sanskrit texts, the city of Pravara emerges as the new capital, replacing the old capital of Puranadhisthana (The Old Site or Capital, in Sanskrit) – modern Pandrethan. Pravarapur and Pandrethan essentially form the royal citadel, encompassing the palace together with major religious sites consecrated by the rulers and the surrounding environs. Together, they constitute a larger geospatial entity: Srinagar, the city. In terms of its geographical location, the city stands almost midway along the slow, meandering course of the Jhelum river. In medieval Sanskrit texts, Kashmir consists of two divisions: Maraz (south, upstream) and Kamraz (north, downstream), with Srinagar located centrally, right on the boundary between the two. The divisions did not follow any geographical feature, and neither did they function as administrative units in the early history of Kashmir. However, they helped orient people, with the city serving as the lodestone of travel and movement. Even today, when most people are ignorant of these past terms, those living in the north refer to their travel to Srinagar as *shahr khasun* (travelling up to the city) while those in the south call it *shahr vasun* (travelling down to the city), reflecting that, in the distant past, the river was the highway, and the city the destination.

In around 631, the Chinese Buddhist monk and traveller Xuanzang (or Hsüen-tsang) arrived in Kashmir. The visit was part of his extensive travels in South Asia to discover and locate Buddhist teachers and texts. In Kashmir, Xuanzang's arrival possibly coincided with the formation of Karkota rule, though we are not sure if the crown had passed to the Karkota dynasty at the time of his arrival. Whatever the case, it seems that the Chinese monk received a warm reception from the king. He records being welcomed by a large assembly comprising the king, courtiers and leading priests, before being escorted into the city in a ceremonial procession, mounted on an exceptionally large elephant. In Kashmir, as expected, Xuanzang spent most of his time discoursing with monks and he also visited Buddhist sites, of which he leaves a brief description. Interestingly, in his memoirs, the city of Pravarapur, although almost a century old at the time of the visit, continued to be referred to as the "new capital". Pravarapur had yet to settle down into the respectability that often comes with age rather than material extravagance and wealth. Even today, cities continue to confound our understanding of life and our place in it: some cities never grow, while some outgrow their initial footprints, almost devouring everything in their way.

For Xuanzang, the new capital was definitively located within a Buddhist milieu, even if it was no longer a Buddhist city: "The capital of this country on the west borders on the Great River. There are 100 religious foundations in it, and about 5000 priests. Moreover, there are four stupas of wonderful height and great magnificence: these were built by Asoka-raja." The Chinese author also writes about Sangharama, a Buddhist monastery located on the spur of the mountain ridge overlooking the city. The monastery was attached to a stupa housing a sacred relic, "a tooth of Buddha in length about an inch and a half, of a yellowish white colour; on religious days it emits a bright light". The location of this stupa, which served as a centre of Buddhist travel into Kashmir during the medieval period, remains untraced.

The association of major monuments in the city with the great benefactor of Buddhism in South Asia, the Mauryan emperor Ashoka (c. 268–232 BCE), also underlines how, before Hun rule, Kashmir was a Buddhist land. Buddhist texts mention that the monk Madhyantika, the last disciple of Ananda (fifth–fourth century BCE), was sent by the emperor to Gandhara and Kashmir. Not only did Madhyantika make Kashmir Buddhist, but he also made the land habitable. Xuanzang also records the legends of Madhyantika regarding the origin of human settlement in Kashmir, which firmly locates the event in Buddhist mythology. This legend was very likely widespread in Kashmir and was later incorporated into Puranic lore in the *Nilamata Purana*, which was produced either during Lalitaditya's time or thereabouts, if not earlier. In this adaptation and reworking of older Buddhist legends, the central characters assume Hindu forms. Madhyantika is replaced by the Hindu sage Kashyap Rishi. The emergence of Kashmir as a habitable land is seen as an act of divine grace, and to mark this celestial intervention the geography of the land is fused with the presence of the entire pantheon of gods and goddesses in Hindu mythology. In a story of intertwined traditions, myths and place-making, the Nilamata Purana provides descriptive sketches of major pilgrimage centres of the land, a narrative repeated in Kalhana's *Rajatarangini*.

Even before the arrival of Xuanzang in Srinagar, Kashmir was attracting the attention of scholars and students from China. Simultaneously, itinerant Kashmiri monks made their way into China, serving as translators of major Buddhist texts. Sometime in the first half of the fourth century, a Buddhist monk, Kumarajiva (d. 413), arrived in Kashmir from Khotan before proceeding to China, where he spent the rest of his life dedicated to the translation of Buddhist texts. About the time when Kumarajiva was in Khotan, a Kashmiri monk, Gunavarman (367–431), made his way to Java, converting the Hindu ruler to Buddhism. Soon he arrived in China at the invitation of Emperor Wen (r. 424–453) of the Liu Song dynasty, and translated many Buddhist works in the capital, Nanking.

Xuanzang also repeats the tale of how the Kushan emperor Kanishka had inscribed the text of *Tripitaka*, an early Buddhist canon, on copper plates and deposited it in a stupa. The stupa remains unidentified to this day, yet the tale of the copper plates has not been forgotten. In the late 1960s, the desire to discover the plates caught the imagination of Ghulam Muhammad Sadiq (d. 1971), the chief minister of the state of Jammu and Kashmir. As is the practice in such state ventures, scholars were asked for their opinions on where to excavate. It is rumoured that Ibn-e Mahjoor, the son of Kashmir's leading modern poet, Pirzada Ghulam Ahmad Mahjoor (d. 1952), made it known that he was aware of the exact location of the hidden plates. But then he named a price for his scholarly labours. Probably the money asked for was too much or maybe Sadiq simply lost interest. After all, even elected leaders, just like kings and emperors, are given to boredom. The popular belief is that the plates are either buried at Ushkara, the Kushan town at the entrance to Kashmir, or in Harwan, in the suburbs of Srinagar.

Centuries after Xuanzang, Kalhana also wrote about the two cities, the old and the new capital. Significantly, where the Buddhist monk only mentions Buddhist edifices in the city patronized by Ashoka, the Kashmiri historian links him with the very foundation of Srinagar as the king who "built the town of Srinagari, which was most important on account of its ninety-six lakhs of houses resplendent with wealth".[1] To date, despite almost a century of archaeological excavations in Kashmir, no

## THE CITY OF PRAVARA

layer of Mauryan presence has been located in Srinagar or, for that matter, in Kashmir. In Kalhana's account, Ashoka is not the great emperor ruling from Patliputra (Patna) but a native Kashmiri king whose claim to fame is based on establishing Srinagar. Was Kashmir a part of the Mauryan Empire? We have no evidence to prove it.

Historically, it was under Kushan rule that Buddhism made inroads into Kashmir, especially under Emperor Kanishka (r. 127–150). At Harwan, on the foothills of the Zabarwan mountains overlooking Srinagar, a series of excavations in the first half of the twentieth century revealed the most significant evidence of Buddhist art and Kushan rule in the region. Ironically, as in most such finds, the discovery was partially linked to the desire to modernize the city. In 1893, Srinagar was provided with tap water, a major improvement in the life of the city, which was prone to periodic outbreaks of cholera due to the consumption of contaminated river water. To improve the water supply, a water reservoir was constructed in the village of Harwan on a perennial stream, the Dachigham-Telbal *nallah*. Sometime around 1895, during the construction of the conduits from the reservoir to the royal palace (and the city at large), a few moulded brick tiles were also discovered, but this did not arouse any special interest at the time. Until thirty years later, when in 1923 a series of mounds in the village of Harwan was excavated, revealing remains of a stupa, an apsidal temple, *vihara* (Buddhist monastery) and additional cells. The excavations also revealed a series of terracotta tiles, used in the pavement around the temple and also on the temple facade. The man behind the excavation, Pandit Ram Chandra Kak, who would also briefly serve as the prime minister of the princely state of Jammu and Kashmir, described the finds:

> the physiognomy and, to some extent, the dress of the men and women are wholly unlike that of any of the races at

> present residing in Kashmir, or for that matter of that in India. Their facial characteristics bear close resemblance to those of the inhabitants of the region around Yarkand and Kashgar [...]
>
> [...] The peculiar interest of the Harwan monuments lies in the fact that they are the only remains of their kind in India (possibly in the world), and that they supply a life-like representation of the features of those mysterious people, the Kushans.[2]

In the 1930s, when Kak was writing his *Ancient Monuments of Kashmir*, the world of the Kushans could feel both distant and "mysterious". However, in the third century, the Kushan Empire extended from Xinjiang in Central Asia to the former Mauryan capital of Patliputra. Originating in the grasslands of northwestern China, the Kushans (or the Yuezhi) would fight, lose and regroup before moving into Bactria, the site of the Graeco-Bactrian kingdoms (256–120 BCE) founded by Alexander's generals. Soon they would emerge as the masters not only of Bactria but Gandhara and areas further east of the vast Gangetic plains. The Kushan Empire was assimilative, a truly cosmopolitan world. Kushan art includes Hellenistic and Sasanian motifs, but that is not the full extent of their artistic traditions or borrowing. The iconography borrows equally from the Chinese, Assyrians and Romans. This coming together of a myriad of cultures can also be seen at Harwan. Viewed in a museum gallery as stand-alone displays, the tiles represent a series of unconnected visual images: a hunting scene depicting the famed Parthian shot, a dragon with a foliate tail and a trunk-like snout, vegetative scrolls of lotus and grape-bearing vines, and a panel with an emaciated ascetic. Somewhere in between stands a graceful dancer dressed in a loose robe and trousers and holding on to a scarf as her sole prop.

# THE CITY OF PRAVARA

The depiction of the subjects varies from fanciful and stylized rendering to scenes that appear realistic. At times, they borrow imagery that seemingly is located in the daily life of the common people—the city people. One could argue that despite their vastly differing subjects, the tiles serve as the visual register of an early stage of urbanization in Kashmir. The scenes of couples engaging in animated conservation seated on balconies with wooden railings call to mind the similar wooden *dubs* (projecting balconies) of old houses in Srinagar today. Such scenes remain commonplace even now, after the passage of more than two millennia. Traditions maintain that Kanishka convened the Fourth Buddhist Council in Kundalavana in Kashmir, leading to the compilation of *Abhidharma Mahavibhasa Sastra* (Great Abhidharma Commentary) a canonical work which would become integral to the Mahayana school of Buddhism. The generally accepted view identifies Kundalavana with Harwan.

The Harwan site, as a place of both artistic production and scholastic disputation, highlights the role of the Kushans not only as consumers but also as producers and transmitters of a knowledge system and artistic tradition. Moreover, it is to this moment that the city of Srinagar owes its first artistic florescence. If not the makers of the Silk Road, the Kushans embodied both the spirit of the movement and the dissemination of human knowledge along the route. The introduction of Buddhism to China is generally credited to them, though the actual process was advanced by the zeal of Buddhist missionaries, monks and, occasionally, merchants. In this process Kashmir also played its part.

Certainly there was an older capital city even before Pravarapur, but how old we cannot guess. And, in popular traditions, Kashmir was linked to the memory of Ashoka. Three miles south of Lal Chowk, the present-day city centre, lies Badami Bagh, a sprawling military cantonment. For some, it marks India's military presence in Srinagar and the region at large. Aside from serving as the nucleus of the military establishment in Kashmir, the cantonment also marks the site of Puranadhisthana, or Pandrethan as it is known today. Within this military complex, set up in the first quarter of the twentieth century under the Dogra regime, the most significant structure today is the temple of Meruvardhanaswami, a tenth-century monument situated within a water tank. Given the prevailing popular penchant for the mongrelization of historical names, and also the picturesque temple setting, some have started to refer to the temple as Pani Mandir, or Water Temple. Inaccessible to people at large, both natives and visitors, the monument is the only medieval stone temple surviving in its entirety in Kashmir. In 1868, when the British photographer John Burke visited Kashmir, he also photographed the monument along with other local historical sites. In a black and white image, he captures the temple standing forlorn within a marshy site, with almost no visible signs of the surrounding water tank.

Aside from the architecture of the temple, which borrows from Greek architectural traditions transmitted through Kushans, of special significance is the geese and duck decoration on the corbelled roof ceiling of the temple. It is possible that not only the ceiling but also the walls were plastered and painted. A polychromatic interior would certainly have added a much-needed splash of colour to the gloomy sanctum. Much as with Greek sculptures with their surface of translucent whiteness, we are used to seeing most medieval temples as monochromatic spaces. In Kashmir, the predominant colour is a drab grey, the colour of both limestone and basalt stone used in constructing these monuments. Sometimes the surface acquires a shiny gleam, owing to erosion or the constant rubbing of hands or feet of worshippers.

## THE CITY OF PRAVARA

The Shree Pratap Singh Museum in Srinagar showcases countless stone sculptures excavated in Kashmir during the twentieth century. While many are sourced from building exteriors and are chiselled in relief, there are numerous examples that are exquisitely finished with a high gloss polish. However, it was only during Muslim rule that the practice of polishing stone for framing architectural elements came into vogue in Kashmir. But dress them with a layer of paint and a different aesthetic appears on the horizon. The museum also houses a series of statutes depicting Bodhisattva, Shiva and Hindu goddesses, some of which date to the eighth century. One of the Bodhisattva statutes still retains traces of lime plaster at the base. A few years back colour pigments painted over the plaster could also be seen, but today it is virtually impossible to locate the paint, even though the accompanying signage still mentions it. This indicates that statues, and similarly the wall surfaces in the temple interiors, were plastered and painted.

Coming back to the temple at Pandrethan, if we were to remove the constraints that limit our imagination and build on the play of colours—the flickering of a golden light from a brass lampstand with its multi-tiered sequence of oil wick lamps—and then add to the visuals the all-pervading aroma of incense, Pani Mandir morphs into something unique. Each additional layer of colour and material that our imagination can suggest builds on the richness of the interiors, recreating the temple almost as it would have been in its heyday. One could argue that this material reimagination accords with the theory of suggestion (*dhvani*) which was central to the Sanskrit aesthetics of medieval Kashmir.

At a walkable distance from the renamed Pani Mandir, within the confines of the cantonment, the Army also maintains an open-air museum. This houses some of the excavated material, including a colossal multi-faceted monolithic Shiv Lingam. In

1913 several cells, remnants of Kashmir's Buddhist heritage, including a monastery (*vihara*) and two stupas, were excavated at the site. Though the Army has spent considerable effort and resources in rehabilitating the Meruvardhanaswami as a functional temple, including the reconstruction of an artificial moat around it, the Buddhist stupa and *vihara* lost out to the numerous military barracks that kept on being erected at the site. It is probable that, the archaeological remains excavated would have appeared fairly insignificant and failed to appeal to the sense of history on the part of officialdom in a major institution like the Army. Aside from what is left in the Badami Bagh cantonment, Puranadhisthana exists only in texts.

Very similar is the case of Pravarapur. The king after whom the new city was named was a sixth-century ruler, Pravarasena II (r. 530–590), from the dynasty that Kalhana refers to as the restored House of Gonanda. Pravarasena was a White Hun (Sveta Huna, in Sanskrit), named after his grandfather Pravarasena I, who also patronized construction in Srinagar at the old capital, Puranadhisthana. Some believe that the Huns are ethnically of Turkish, Turco-Mongol or Iranian origin. It is most probable that they were a mixture of all three and possibly more, forming a political confederacy rather than a single ethnic unit, as Hyun Jin Kim describes them in *The Huns*.

Unlike their European counterparts, who gained a great degree of infamy owing to the raids of Attila the Hun (r. 434–453) on the Roman Empire, the White Huns hardly find any mention in popular history or memory, even in the lands they once ruled. For two centuries, they were the paramount power in Central Asia, with their empire extending into the northern and western parts of South Asia. Beginning in the fourth century, the Huns spread into Europe, Central Asia and South Asia from their ancestral land, a vast geographical territory that included Central Asia (the five Central Asian republics and Afghanistan), almost all of what is now southern Russia from western Siberia to the Pacific Ocean in the Far East, all of modern Mongolia, and large portions of northern and western China.

Supplanting the Gupta Empire (c. 320–550), they made the fertile plains of Punjab the centre of their empire, with modern Sialkot as their probable capital. By the sixth century, a secondary king of the Huns, Toramana, made inroads further south into mainland India; he is seen as the first Hun king of India. Kashmir was conquered along with present-day Rajasthan, Uttar Pradesh, and the lands down to Madhya Pradesh. Though the centre of his kingdom was located in the west, in the Gandhara region, Kashmir remained an important territory of the Hun Empire. Significantly the White Huns served as promoters of the cult of Shiva. Mihirakula, the son and successor of Toramana, is remembered in Buddhist texts as a great tormentor of the people of the Buddhist faith. Mihirakula's cruelty finally resulted in a rebellion and his dethronement; losing his main territories in the plains, he retreated to Kashmir.

The Gwalior inscription, a dedicatory epigraph made for a sun temple in Gwalior, opens with verses in praise of Mihirakula, highlighting the Hun investment in Hinduism from an early time. In Kashmir, it was under the Huns that we see the slow demise of Buddhism, corresponding with the development of the cult of Shiva. Mihirakula is remembered for destroying Buddhist sites and massacring a large number of the Buddhist community, both monks and commoners. Though some blame the Hun king for the near-total erasure of Buddhist sites in Kashmir, this is not true. Xuanzang's description indicates that Buddhist sites continued to exist and were venerated across the sacred landscape of medieval Kashmir, even at a later date. For Kalhana, Mihirakula was a "perverse-minded" tormentor of both humans and animals, notwithstanding his military exploits and distribution of largesse to the Brahmins. The king's patronage included endowing the Brahmins of Gandhara with extensive land grants (*agraharas*) in Kashmir. For Mihirakula, this scheme served a twin purpose: to recreate a semblance of his old court and as a practical endeavour to encourage the Hindu priestly class to relocate to the Himalayan kingdom, thereby effectively reshaping Kashmir as a Hindu land.

The sixth century marks both the high point of Hun dominance and the eventual collapse of the Hun Empire at the hands of a confederacy of Turks and Persians led by the Sasanians. Thereafter, they would survive as regional kingdoms: the restored House of Gonanda in Kashmir; and at Kabul and Gandhara as the Turk Shahis (and later as the Hindu Shahis). Centuries later they would re-emerge on the political map of South Asia as a ruling power, this time as the progenitors of two new dynasties, both Muslim: the Shahmiri Sultanate (1339–1561) in Kashmir, and the Khilji Sultanate (1290–1320) of Delhi.

The Kashmir of Pravarasena was Hun territory: the making of an independent Kashmiri geography was yet to take place. That happened at a later date, under Lalitaditya and his successors. Very little evidence is available of how the city of Pravara looked, for there is hardly any archaeological trace. A few stones, remnants of the entrance gateway to a temple, can be found near the northeastern corner of Srinagar's oldest surviving Muslim cemetery, Mazar-i Kalan (The Big Cemetery). These provide a small, tantalizing insight into the architecture of the city. But the city does find brief mention in many Sanskrit texts, some authored decades after rulership had passed away from Hindu kings. The seventeenth-century Kashmiri poet and scribe Ratnakantha in his colophon on *Devistotra*, a Sanskrit work produced in Kashmir, celebrates the city of Pravara as the site where two rivers, Doodh Ganga and Jhelum, meet: "Where the Goddess blessed the Pradyumna Hill with the form of Śarikā, where the river of the Goddess of Destruction and the river arising from the eyes of the boar meet, where the king named Pravara went in bodily form to Mount Kailasa."[3]

In one of his most famous passages describing the city, Kalhana also writes about the towering twelve-storey mansions in the city and overflowing markets. Even today, while most buildings of historic Srinagar, especially along the riverfront, engage with the horizontal scale, comprising three or four floors, there are still a few residences in the city that are five or six floors high. In certain cases, given the sloping roof designs, some houses have specially designed wooden pavilions surmounting the actual roofline. These small airy wooden pavilions, famously referred to as *zoon dubs* (moon pavilions), provide a panoramic view of the city, and also add a floor or two to the building's height. Still, given the present scale of the historic building fabric, imagining a city with streets filled with twelve-storey-high mansions seems more of a poetic fancy than a material reality. Far more realistic is the description of Xuanzang. About the general size of the city, he writes: "It [the capital] is from north to south 12 or 13 li [3.5–4 miles], and from east to west 4 or 5 li [1–1.5 miles]."[4] Xuanzang's measurements roughly agree with what we know of the greatest extent the city occupied on the right bank of the Jhelum, before the modern expansions of the twentieth century. When the European traveller George Forster (d. 1792) arrived in Srinagar during the spring of 1783, he also described the city extending three miles on either side of the Jhelum, with private gardens and open fields on its east and west.

Earlier, another medieval Sanskrit poet, Bilhana who, after leaving Kashmir, achieved fame at the court of the Chalukya king Vikramaditya VI (r. 1076–1126), also offers an insight into the daily life of the city. Writing in the heat of the Indian plains, Bilhana reminisces about the plentiful bathing houses located on the Jhelum, which provided the bathers with hot water during the freezing winter months—a sure sign of luxury and civilization:

And boat-borne bathhouses at the Vitasta's shore
Each in their abundance during the winter months
Point to the pleasure of heaven.[5]

Interesting as they may be, these textual references are hardly adequate for understanding how Pravarasena's city looked and how it functioned. The river Jhelum must have been a major feature of the city, but what about the roads and the streets? Was the city characterized by a regular layout aligned in a certain direction? Did it possess any main road leading to the palace and the principal religious sites? How, then, were the political, residential, religious and commercial areas of the city marked? Were they separated, or did they constitute a homogenized whole, with the different structures interwoven? We simply have no way of imagining the urban programme that dictated the architecture of the city.

The *Nilamata Purana* speaks about well-laid roads in the city, the main ones intersecting in four ways, leading to the formation of plazas. This seems to indicate a rectangular layout similar to what we find in the Bronze Age cities of Mohenjo-daro and Harappa. The presence of straight parallel streets is also seen in towns in Gandhara and cities established by the Kushans. Occasionally, the Kushans also followed the earlier tradition of having the royal palace in a citadel, separated from the main city. At Pravarapur, the palace occupied an elevated terrain, the foothills of the Hari Parbat, commanding a fine view of the city, the Jhelum and the approaches to the city. This proved a prudent planning decision. Unlike many medieval cities, Srinagar was not walled. The city was ringed by a series of water bodies connected to the Jhelum, not a man-made moat or citadel. The rulers of Kashmir seemed to be impervious to the need to fortify the capital, and more than once the belief in the natural protection provided by the waterways proved mistaken.

## THE CITY OF PRAVARA

Kalhana's text does indicate that the approach to the city was defended by manned city gates. Revolts and insurrections in the kingdom usually made their way to these gates before descending into looting, mayhem and arson. It seems safe to posit that the gates would have been located on the main routes of approach, possibly at the location of the boat bridges, to stop the enemy advance and guard entry into the city. However, there is nothing in medieval texts that would help us in locating the city gates.

Kalhana also speaks about four gates in the city, known as the Lion Gates (Siṃhadvar), based on their iconography. One of the gates also framed the entrance to the royal palace. Though the gates could have been carved out of wood, there is a far greater possibility that they were built from the same massive limestone blocks that line the colossal entrance portals to the temple complex at Martand and Awantipur. The imagery of a lion on the gateway seems to have been common. It was also found on either side of the entrance gateway to the Bijbehara Temple (c. fifth century). While this temple gateway no longer exists, John Siudmak, in his magisterial work on the sculptures of Kashmir, describes one of the surviving lions from the gateway depicted sejant. Seated lions atop twin stone columns can also be seen on terracotta plaques excavated from Harwan.

During the reign of Harsha (r. 1089–1101), the king had a large bell hung from each of the four gates so that common people could gain his attention. The innovation, it seems, drew the public, and crowds gathered near the gates in the hope of obtaining an audience with the king. Centuries later, and in a different land, the Mughal emperor Jahangir (r. 1605–1627) instituted a similar system for dispensing justice, by placing a chain of justice outside his palace.

The palace gates were also a major site for staging spectacles, not all of which were pleasant. During the chaotic last years of

Harsha's reign, these gates carried the severed heads of rebel nobles—the infamous Damaras. For those arriving at the palace, this passage must have served as a grim reality check. Similarly, during an extreme case of famine when the citizenry along with the nobles carried out a mass insurrection, Harsha had the heads of the captured rebels impaled on pikes lining the main streets of the city. The king's fate mirrored that of the rebels. He became the first king of Kashmir to be beheaded, his head being affixed to a pike. Kings following Harsha drowned their enemies in the water of the Jhelum, the feet of the condemned being tied to a boulder, just in case the river proved inadequate for the task. In the nineteenth century, the Dogra rulers would hang convicts from the bridge in the heart of the city, leaving the corpses exposed for days in a gruesome public spectacle.

Tragic as the king's end may have been, it did result in the production of *Katha Sarit Sagara* (Ocean of the Streams of Stories) by the court poet Somadeva to console Harsha's grief-ridden mother, Queen Suryavati. This epic, an abridgment of a much older work called *Brhatkatha*, is believed to have been written somewhere around 1063–1081. While not the greatest literature of Kashmir, it does nevertheless serve as an anthology of myths, legends, quasi-historical events and fantastic occurrences that not only constituted the folk memory of medieval Kashmir but also marked a field of literary interest for aesthetes such as Somadeva. The stories are crafted from religious and secular subjects to draw laughter, something we can assume a distraught Suryavati would have needed. Four centuries later, when Kashmir was a Muslim land, the work was translated into Persian as *Bahr al-Asmar* (Ocean of Stories). In addition, some of the stories from the collection made their way into a fourteenth-century Persian work, *Tuti Nama*. Written by the Persian Sufi poet Ziya al-Din Nakhshabi on his arrival in India, *Tuti Nama* served as the subject for the first major *muraqqa* (illuminated album)

# THE CITY OF PRAVARA

to be produced in the Mughal atelier under the patronage of Emperor Akbar (r. 1556–1605). Today, this artwork continues to be practised in South Asia, labelled somewhat erroneously as Mughal miniature paintings. In Kashmir, scenes from the *Tuti Nama* occasionally made their way into decorative panels of papier mâché.

Despite the chaos that engulfed Kashmir under Harsha, Kalhana's detailed account of his reign helps us to understand how the city was shaping on the eve of Muslim rule in Kashmir. For the poet-historian, Harsha remains an iconoclast; a shameless, idle, evil ruler, who desecrated temples and committed sacrileges against the idols residing in them. He addresses the king as Tursuka—the Turk. The king, according to Kalhana, was attended by a hundred Tursukas. Some scholars note that this marks the presence of Muslim Turks in the city.

Harsha favoured Parihaspur rather than Srinagar as his capital. The unlucky king also built a colossal palace, rectangular in plan, with a rumoured hundred doors. The shape of the building and the numerous doors leading to it are specially recorded by Kalhana, indicating that this was an innovation and not the norm. The exact location of his palace remains untraced, but in all probability it was in Srinagar and not Parihaspur. The main entrance to the palace was from the Lion Gate and led into a series of courtyards. A separate gate led away from the city towards the surrounding villages—an escape route. These courtyards served as the locations for elaborate royal ceremonies and equally grim battles. The responsibility for the security and functioning of the royal palace (*rajasthana*) was overseen by a governor who enjoyed privileges similar to that of the city's custodian.

Medieval Sanskrit texts are uniformly silent about the urban working force. Who were these people? In the reign of Harsha, we have a faint indication that immigrant Muslim Turks were increasingly settling in the city, not only as mercenaries in court service but also as iterant merchants and, more importantly, as artisans. Around the time Harsha was ruling, a group of unnamed artisans from Kashmir arrived in Alchi, in Ladakh, participating in the construction and embellishment of many Buddhist temples.

The foundation of the temple in Alchi is popularly credited to a revered eleventh-century monk, Rinchen Zangpo (958–1055). Early in his life, Zangpo is said to have arrived in Kashmir, where he studied with Buddhist teachers. On his return to Ladakh, according to legend, he was accompanied by thirty-two Kashmiri artisans, who were responsible for constructing a series of temples there, fifty-one to be precise. Modern scholars differ about the details; the date commonly suggested for the site varies from the twelfth to the middle of the thirteenth century. At Alchi, the series of Buddhist wooden temples erected by the artisans represent the oldest extant form of Kashmiri wooden architecture. Wooden porticos (*dalan*, in Kashmiri), much weathered today, precede the temples at the site, of which the most impressive is to be found at the Sumtsek Temple. The *dalan* at Sumtsek takes the shape of an impressive two-storey wooden colonnade. The detailing of the *dalan* with its fluted wooden columns, the iconography of human and mythical figures in a quintessential semicircular profile based on three arches (thus the name trefoil), the vegetative scrolls, and the chequered chessboard motif uniquely tie the buildings to the architectural predilections of medieval Kashmir. The carved rectangular pilasters and architraves seen in medieval stone temples of Kashmir have been faithfully copied and recreated in wood at Alchi. Significantly the Sumtsek Temple also retains the artwork of painters from Kashmir on the *dhoti* (loincloth) of the presiding deity, an eighteen-foot-tall statute of Avalokiteshvara. Given the difficulties of preserving the artwork, photography is strictly prohibited inside the temple.

## THE CITY OF PRAVARA

The iconography in the temple interiors of Alchi shows myriad influences, not limited to the geographical boundaries of Ladakh or Kashmir alone. We find riders shooting arrows—the typical Parthian shot—dressed in gowns (*aba*) and loose pants (*yazar*), and wearing a turban (*dastar*). The borders of the tunic are in *tiraz*, the inscribed textile in fashion at the court of the Fatimid and Abbasid caliphs. Serving as a robe of honour (*khilat*), they were bestowed upon those who had served the interests of the caliph, as well as visiting ambassadors from friendly courts. Initially, the inscriptions on the *tiraz* textiles were in Kufi script, but at a later date, with the development of *thuluth* and *naskh* scripts, these were also included. At Alchi, one can see a pseudo-Kufi text serving a purely decorative function. So who were the artists who included subjects heavily indebted to Muslim culture on the walls of Alchi? If, as tradition maintains, they were indeed Kashmiri artists, then it seems obvious that the visual iconography represented a cultural practice prevalent at the court of the kings of Kashmir. Or else the artisans were not native Kashmiri, but Tursukas of Kalhana's narrative. Either way, the Kashmir of Harsha and his successors was increasingly open to people (including artisans) from Central Asia, some of whom were Muslims of Turkish origin.

We know that the kings of Kashmir prized elephants, which were specially acquired from mainland India. Harsha once rewarded the court musician Bhimanayaka with a pair of elephants. Certainly it was not the best gift, in view of the care that was involved, but then promenading in the streets on the back of an elephant must have appealed to the vanity of the poet. And, as a tribe, poets do tend to be a bit vain. But elephants cannot be paraded in narrow streets and alleys, which again seems to indicate that at least the principal approaches and streets of the city would have followed a more geometrical layout, as mentioned in the Nilamata Purana. The city also had a system of open drains, discharging into the Jhelum. During the tumultuous twelfth century, when Srinagar saw three kings on the throne within the space of a night and a day, the bodies of the rebels were disposed of in the open drain.

Along the streets of the city, to the side, you would occasionally find miniature temples—scaled-down versions of the originals. Placed on top of fluted stone columns of human height, from a distance they would appear quite statuesque despite their diminutive size. Today, a few isolated remnants of these columns can still be observed in the city and continue to be part of the ritual of daily life. On the road leading to Naushera, one such surviving column is still used to feed birds: a handful of rice grains are sprinkled daily on the top of the column by a shopkeeper. Another now functions as a pillar of illumination at a shrine, with niches carved into the sides to house candles. The few miniature temples that survive today are displayed in the city museum. Apart from the routine of day-to-day rituals, these columns could also work as props for a more dramatic spectacle. During the reign of one of Kashmir's most illustrious rulers, Sultan Zain al-Abidin (r. 1420–1470), an unnamed yogi, in a manner reminiscent of the Christian monk Simeon Stylites (d. 459), climbed on top of a tall column in the city. After he had meditated for nine days with eyes closed and without taking a drop of water, his penance resulted in the birth of a son to the sultan.

Returning to medieval Srinagar, the murder of Harsha neither fully restored order nor brought much-desired peace and stability to the city. Brief interludes of peace were overshadowed by an equally swift descent into a cycle of chaos. In a land where fathers feared their sons, parricide became common. Pretenders roamed the city streets in two-horse chariots, a privilege once reserved for royalty. A small land, torn by internal dissensions, gradually consumed all its hoarded riches. In the absence of surplus materials or resources, cities tend to survive through

# THE CITY OF PRAVARA

self-cannibalization, and so it happened in Srinagar. The city was repeatedly surrounded and attacked by rebels, charging on horses coloured with vermilion, as if anticipating the bloodbath to come. Entire neighbourhoods were lost, and the city itself burned, again and again. Royal gardens on the outskirts were stripped of trees, which were consumed by invading armies as firewood. Women in the royal harem watched the mayhem and approaching death from the rooftops of their palace. At times, to save the city, the city guardians had the boat bridges removed, along with the bathhouses praised by Kalhana. But its doom was ineluctable, and destruction came from an unexpected quarter. The Mongols were on their way to Srinagar.

# 4

MONGOLS AND TURKS

*A Turk by the name of Zilchu, with 70,000 Turks from Turkistan, entered Kashmir from the Baramulah road and started spilling the blood [of the people] and pillaging and destroying [the land] and, with tyranny and oppression, brought to an end the lives of most of the inhabitants of this country. They killed several thousand people.*

                Haider Malik Chadurah, *Tarikh-i Kashmir*

*When the violence caused by the Rakshasa Dalcha ceased, the son found not his father, nor the father his son, nor did brothers meet their brothers. Kashmira became almost like a region before creation, a vast field with few men, without food, and full of grass.*

                    Pandit Jonaraja, *Rajatarangini*

NOT MUCH IS KNOWN about the man who would devastate Kashmir, despoil the land, and inadvertently inaugurate a change in the political structure of Kashmir. The raid of Zilchu (or Dalcha) was a brief one, occurring over the summer of 1320. The stay of the invaders was cut short by the approach of early winter. Many Kashmiri sources speak about how the invading army, along with captured Kashmiris, perished on the road as Zilchu's army tried to make its way back home. But who was Zilchu, and was he of Turkish origin or a Mongol? The Sanskrit historian Jonaraja does not mention a Mongol presence in Kashmir, and most Muslim historians who followed him are also silent about any Mongol intrusion into Kashmir.

Nevertheless, the anonymous author of *Baharistan-i Shahi* (c. 1614) does indicate that the invading army was a mix of Mongol and Turkish troops.[1] Medieval Kashmiri historians seem to have developed a special interest in describing the past based on memory, as distinct from actual history. This is a tradition of history writing that was inherited and further perfected by Muslim historians of Kashmir.

Around the time when Zilchu's invasion is said to have taken place, a Persian, a Jewish convert to Islam, Khwaja Rashid al-Din Hamdani (d. 1318), was writing his *Jami al-Tawarikh* (c. 1300–1310).[2] The work serves as a general history of the world, but its significance lies in the detailed account it provides of Mongol rule. *Jami al-Tawarikh* was composed at the Mongol Ilkhan court, where Rashid al-Din served as a vizier under sultans Ghazan (r. 1295–1304) and Uljaytu (r. 1304–1316). The Ilkhanate was established in and around present-day Iran by Genghis Khan's grandson Hulegu Khan (r. 1256–1265). Subservient to the Great Khan, Hulegu had earlier despoiled Baghdad, killing the last Abbasid caliph, al-Mustasim (r. 1242–1258). Under Ghazan, Islam was made the state religion, and the sultan himself converted to Islam, though the court was characterized by a spirit of religious tolerance. According to Rashid al-Din, Sultan Ghazan could speak Kashmiri in addition to many other languages. Rashid al-Din's history also has a chapter on India, one of the main informants for which was a Kashmiri Buddhist monk, Kamalashri.

Importantly, Rashid al-Din writes about the presence of a Mongol *tamma* (garrison) in Kashmir, which was summoned by Hulegu Khan to shore up his power base in Iran. Under the Mongols, *tamma* served as garrison troops stationed in distant frontier territories. The Kashmir *tamma* owed its origin to the command of Hulegu's elder brother, the Great Khan, Mongke Khan (r. 1251–1259), who, according to Rashid al-Din, ordered his general Sali Noyan into Kashmir. About the Mongol intrusion into Kashmir, Rashid al-Din writes: "Sali Noyan took his army to Hindustan and Kashmir, conquered many territories, got much plunder, and sent many Indian slaves to Hulegu Khan. Most of the Indians who are now in *enchu* villages are remnants of them."[3] That most of the captured slaves were from Kashmir is recorded in a separate passage, where Rashid al-Din credits Sali Noyan: "It was he who took Kashmir and brought out several thousand captives."[4] On the basis of his Mongol sources, Rashid al-Din separately records an earlier Mongol raid into Kashmir, under the command of Hoqatur in 1235.[5]

Coming back to Zilchu's raid, the author of *Baharistan-i Shahi* provides a more detailed picture of the event: "Men were killed; women and children were made prisoners and sold to the merchants and traders of Cathay, who had accompanied his troops. All the buildings of the city and the villages [of Kashmir] were burnt [...] These alien troops resorted to indiscriminate bloodshed, killing, and pillaging beyond all limits for a period of eight months [...] Though two hundred and seventy years have elapsed, every stretch of uncultivated and unattended land even now is traced to that period. Hence the saying: 'Here Zilchu cultivated the turf.'"[6] The bleakness and devastation are depicted in a single line by the historian Malik Haidar: "They came, killed, carried and went away."[7]

At this crucial juncture, it was the son of a Tibetan (or Ladakhi) chieftain, Rinchana, who came to the rescue of the people of Kashmir, while the king, Suhadev, fled to the surrounding mountainous region of Kishtwar. Earlier, Rinchana, a Buddhist, had taken refuge at Srinagar, fleeing from his rivals in Tibet. In the aftermath of the invasion, he, with his Tibetan entourage, mounted a successful attack on Srinagar, capturing the already destroyed capital. The ease with which this was achieved indicates how devastated Kashmir was. Rinchana then mediated peace with the leading nobles at the court, marrying Kota Rani, the daughter of Suhadev's army chief.

Nominally, Kashmir once again had a Buddhist king, Rinchana (r. 1320–1322), but this was soon to change. The new king took his residence in the *mohalla* of Dedhmar, on the right bank. This neighbourhood had been established by Queen Didda (Dedhi Rein, in Kashmiri), and following the practice in medieval Kashmir, it took the name of its founder. Didda had ruled Kashmir (r. 980–1003)[8] with a strong hand and a degree of ruthlessness that Kashmir had not witnessed before. She eliminated her grandchildren and numerous courtiers to secure her reign. Despite facing fierce opposition and multiple rebellions from discontented nobles, she endured, ultimately dying peacefully in bed and passing the throne to a new dynasty, the House of Lohara. Historically, three women ruled Kashmir, but Didda was the most successful, triumphing in a male-dominated and violent world. From what historians have written, it emerges that the queen had an equally colourful personal life; she took numerous paramours for pleasure as well as to secure her throne. For this indiscretion, she has received a bad press. On account of her lameness, Kalhana occasionally refers to her as the lame queen or, after the death of her husband, as the widowed queen. The view of Kalhana towards the queen's supposedly promiscuous behaviour is reflective of a general attitude found in medieval texts in which the blame for any societal decay or unravelling of order is often placed on women or people of low standing: the poor, those engaged in menial jobs, the most disenfranchised and powerless. In the world of Kalhana, a woman is inclined by her very nature to fail and fall into a moral abyss: "Alas! The course of women even of noble descent moves by nature downwards, like that of rivers!"[9]

Didda's actual life, nonetheless, was quite successful. In all, she remained the real power behind the throne for forty-five years, which was quite remarkable for anyone, man or woman. The foundation of Dedhmar was occasioned by the death of Didda's son, King Abhimanyu (r. 958–972). This untimely death resulted in a year of mourning before the queen resumed her old "lusting for pleasure", as Kalhana puts it.[10] Notwithstanding how past and present historians may judge her, Didda's legacy endures in Kashmir, and her name Dedh is often still used to refer to any grand old lady, the wise woman of the family, one who is *jahan deedha* (worldly-wise). Within the city, the queen also established a *matha* (Hindu monastery) at Dedhmar in the year of her mourning, the edifice proving as transient as her sorrow. Today a few stones from the *matha* can be seen in the high retaining wall along the Jhelum, providing a measure of safety to the citizens from the floodwaters of the river.

At the time when Rinchana took up residence in Dedhmar, a small Muslim community also resided in a narrow lane of the neighbourhood. Like many such places in Kashmir, the quarter retains its old Sanskrit name, though somewhat corrupted with time: Melchimar (originally, Mleechamar), the quarter of the *mlechchhas* (foreigners). Persian sources are unanimous in recording that one day, early in the morning, the king saw an elderly Muslim offering *nimaz* near the *ghat* (steps down to the river). In later writings, the Muslim is presented as a Sufi, the earliest records mention his name as Baba Bulbul. Rinchana enquired of Baba Bulbul who he was and where he came from. To which Bulbul answered, "I am a stranger." Impressed by the simplicity of the stranger's conduct, the king adopted his faith. Rinchana became Sultan Sadr al-Din, the first Muslim sultan of Kashmir. The occasion is certainly serendipitous: the meeting of two strangers in a foreign land, within a devastated city on the banks of a river that had been witness to a past both glorious and full of infamy. In the burnt-out city, Rinchana laid the foundation of a new quarter, Rinchanapur. Given the recent disturbances, which also included a failed insurrection, the sultan had the royal quarters surrounded by a moat.

Historically, Rinchanapur marks the first known case where the royal quarter, including the palace, was relocated near the river in Srinagar. The construction of a moat around Rinchanapur was a cost-effective measure to secure the royal quarter in case of a revolt. Located on the right bank, near Aali Kadal, the moat no longer survives. Persian sources also write about a royal mosque that Rinchana constructed in the vicinity of the palace. A later generation of Muslim historians would proclaim the mosque of Rinchana as the first Jamia, the Friday Mosque of Kashmir. Today, this first Muslim building of worship constructed by a Kashmiri ruler still survives on the banks of the Jhelum. A small, nondescript structure, it marks Islam's presence in both Srinagar and the sultanate of Kashmir. The idea that the mosque was a large structure befitting its role as the first mosque in Kashmir is belied by both the site's topography and existing archaeological traces.

Rinchana also constructed a *khanqah* for Baba Bulbul, and on his death in 1322, the elderly Muslim, now the royal preceptor, was buried near it. Adjoining the *khanqah*, a free open kitchen (*langer*) operated, feeding the hungry in the city and also introducing the Hindu and Buddhist population to a new religion, Islam. The entire neighbourhood is today known as Bulbul Lanker, in honour of a saint whose origin and actual history remain obscure. For Kashmiri Muslims, Baba Bulbul, or, as he is known today, Bulbul Shah, is the saint who inaugurated Islam in Kashmir and was instrumental in laying the foundation of Muslim rule in the region.

In his successful bid for power, Rinchana was assisted by another immigrant at the court, Shah Mir. Not much is known about Shah Mir's ancestry, but the predominant view seems to be that he was of Turkish origin. A Muslim merchant or soldier for hire, hailing from the mountain region of Swat, in present-day Pakistan, Shah Mir emerged as the leader of a small but significant community of Turkish Muslims in Kashmir. He was responsible for negotiating the withdrawal of an invading army of Turkish or Mongol soldiers. Again, we are not sure who sent these soldiers, but the intent of the invaders seems to have been one of looting rather than permanent conquest.

Meantime, the widowed queen remarried, and fate rendered her a widow again. In trying to mirror Didda, she ascended the royal throne, but the sands of fate had already shifted. Much like Mary, Queen of Scots, destiny had marked her for tragedy, not glory. And so it came to be that Kota Rani was besieged in the fort of Anderkote some fifteen miles northwest of Srinagar and deposed by Shah Mir in 1334. Her final years remain a bit murky. Writing in the court of Shah Mir's great-great-grandson, Pandit Jonaraja provides us with the earliest account of Kota Rani's end. The queen believed in Shah Mir's promise to share the throne and country with her, and married the Turk. The wedding took place, but the next day the queen found herself discarded and imprisoned. Jonaraja does not dwell upon her actual death, but in all probability she was murdered in prison.

There are other, differing accounts of the queen's final moments, some portraying her as a heroic figure who refused to yield to Shah Mir's demands. In these texts, Kota Rani kills herself on her wedding night. In present-day Kashmir, Kota Rani's demise remains a marker of division and contesting narratives. Did she marry, or did she kill herself? For some, she is the last Hindu ruler of Kashmir, who, by rejecting the advances of her erstwhile Muslim suitor, established the glory of her faith. In her heroic death, the reputation of the community stands vindicated.[11] In reality, the queen had already married a Buddhist who then converted to Islam, and after his death she remarried, this time to a Hindu. Thus, for the historical Kota

Rani, the faith of her husband was inconsequential; what was paramount was her survival, her rule. Unfortunately, Kota Rani had neither the luck nor the resources of Didda.

A man of great fortitude, perseverance and ambition, Shah Mir established the first Muslim ruling dynasty of Kashmir, the Shahmiri sultans (r. 1339–1561). The early Shahmiris followed an obscure tradition practised on certain occasions in the Karkota and Lohara dynasties. This involved succession through brothers, rather than the law of primogeniture, and it was in practice till the accession of Sultan Sikandar (r. 1389–1413).[12] Following the Shahmiris, the Chaks (r. 1561–1589), who overthrew the house of Shah Mir, also followed this tradition. As the sultans of Kashmir consolidated their power and the land began to recover from the ravages of Zilchu, the city re-emerged as a cosmopolis, situated at the intersection of the Indic and Persianate worlds. Caravans of itinerant mystics and missionaries, Sufis and *ulema*, accompanied by groups of artisans producing various crafts, made momentous journeys across the treacherous mountainous routes into Srinagar. This influx created a unique habitus in the city, characterized by a distinct Muslim identity rooted in Persian culture. From Shah Mir's accession to the throne as Sultan Shams al-Din (r. 1339–1342) until the end of Muslim rule in Kashmir in the nineteenth century, Srinagar was known by its Persian name: Shahr-i Kashmir (The City of Kashmir).

# 5

# SHAHR-I KASHMIR

> *I bear the flame of unfulfilled love,*
> *Does my grief please you, O Lord?*
>
> Habba Khatun, reputedly Queen<br>of Kashmir, sixteenth century

WHAT MAKES AN INDIVIDUAL traverse great lengths to move to an alien city? Often, we measure such decisions by the material advantages that make such a movement possible and, in certain cases, necessary. Given modern sensibilities that seek to render the role of religion invisible, we tend to underestimate the role of faith in such decisions. In the seventh century, Srinagar witnessed such a migration, of people from the Gangetic plains, to the city in an effort by the rulers from the Karkota dynasty to make Kashmir a Hindu land.[1] Seven centuries later Kashmir would witness another arrival of people, this time from lands to the west of Kashmir, who would gradually transform Srinagar into a Muslim city and the area into a Muslim land.

Across Srinagar, one encounters numerous shrines and cemeteries dedicated to the memory of holy personages. Upon inquiry, it is often found that many of the deceased saints can be traced to a region that was once part of the Persian-speaking world. Mostly dating to the sixteenth and seventeenth centuries, these countless Muslim sacred sites define a pivotal moment in Kashmir's history. They represent the arrival of the last major and hugely successful proselytizing caravan in the city. The continuing reverence these sacred spaces evoke in present-day Srinagar is testimony to the enduring legacy and success of their mission.

Many of these immigrants were Turks (or even Turkomans), though they were invariably rooted in Persianate culture. Given the deep hostility and competition between the modern nation-states of Saudi Arabia, Turkey and Iran, it is remarkable how centuries ago Turks with Persian cultural moorings helped in spreading the faith of Arabia not only in Kashmir but across much of northern India.

Some of those new arrivals in Srinagar hailed from even more distant lands. The oldest mosque in Kashmir, which retains its original architectural character, was constructed by a saint from Arabia: from Medina, the city of the Prophet Muhammad. The epigraph on the mosque wall, recently deciphered by a colleague, Mehran Qureshi, reads: "This mosque was constructed by *faqir* Muhammad al-Madni, a resident of Kashmir, in the year eight hundred and forty-eight of the Hijri."[2]

Upon arrival, most, if not all, of them settled in the capital city. The various Sufi orders, the Kubrawiyya, Suhrawardiyya, Nurbakshiyya and the Naqshbandiyya, all built *khanqahs* in the capital. In the sacred landscape of both the city and the region, these *khanqahs* remain unsurpassed in terms of both their monumental character and their significance in the daily life of a significant population within the Muslim community.

In the early years of the Shahmiri sultanate, Kashmir remained an isolated land: the Mongol ravages were too recent, and the land had yet to stabilize. This would only change in the last quarter of the fourteenth century, under the fourth sultan of the Shahmiri dynasty, Shihab al-Din (r. 1354–1373). After Lalitaditya, Shihab al-Din would prove to be another successful military leader who helped in expanding the physical limits of the *mulk-i Kashmir*. According to Malik Haidar, what proved highly consequential in Shihab al-Din's success was a programme of internal revival and centralization of authority, inaugurated under the sultanate: "Until the period of the Sultans, loyalty did not exist, although some of them paid tributes and taxes that were acceptable to the ruler of the city [...] He turned the country into one strong fort, within a short period."³

Following earlier medieval Kashmiri historians, who in their reports have vastly exaggerated the actual achievements and conquests of past kings, Persian historians have also painted an image of Shihab al-Din as an all-conquering monarch, whose new territories included Badakhshan, Kashgar, Kabul, Punjab and Ladakh. The actual conquest was more limited, but it did include surrounding hill principalities on Kashmir's border, regions in the plains of Punjab, and, more importantly, Ladakh and Baltistan to Kashmir's north.

The arrival of the Kashmiri army in the plains of South Asia must have created a stir, though it went unrecorded in contemporary texts outside Kashmir. For it was in the aftermath of the sultan's conquest that a Sufi shaykh arrived in Srinagar. Future generations of Kashmiri Muslims would hail him as the flag-bearer of Islam in Kashmir, the *baniye-i Musalmani* (the founder of Muslimness). He would be associated not only with a faith but also with the culture that continues to define Kashmir even today. Kashmiris, that is Kashmiri Muslims, popularly call him Shah-i Hamdan (the King of Hamdan), but history remembers him as Mir Sayyid Ali Hamdani (1314–1385), the fourth shaykh in the Kubrawiyya order of Sufis.

# 6

## KHANQAH-I MAULA

*The foundation and the structure of the khanqah as laid by Amir Sayyid Hamdani made it small and limited. Private houses of the inhabitants [of the locality] and the caretakers were so close to the walls of the khanqah that if a fire had broken out in the locality, its flames would engulf the entire khanqah [complex].*

Anonymous, *Baharistan-i Shahi*

TWO DECADES AGO, THE skyline of Srinagar was dominated by the pyramidal spires of the many shrines and mosques towering over the surrounding houses. Today, even more numerous towers of cellular network companies do the same. On a winter morning, after a snowfall, when the sky clears, the riverfront with the Khanqah-i Maula presents a beautiful spectacle—a moment of picturesqueness and cinematic glory.

Some twenty years before a Muslim sultanate was established in Kashmir, in far-away Iran, a new empire of the Ilkhanate was carved out of the Great Mongol Empire of Genghis Khan, the largest contiguous empire humans have ever assembled and one unlikely to be surpassed. As we saw earlier, the Ilkhan court in Iran was characterized by a host of cross-cultural encounters, attracting scholars from Central Asia, Tibet and South Asia. These included Buddhist scholars from Kashmir. Rashid al-Din's *Jami* opens with a chapter on the history of India, Sind and Kashmir. The Kashmiri scholars provided much-needed information about the land.

Also at the Ilkhanate court, we find Ala al-Dawla Simnani (d. 1336), a Kubrawiyya shaykh, engaged in an encounter with Buddhist sages from Kashmir. The engagement occurred in the assembly of the Ilkhanid ruler Argun Khan (1284–1291), near the city of Tabriz, in Iran. In his autobiographical work, Simnani writes about this religious disputation. A few decades later, Simnani's nephew Mir Sayyid Ali Hamdani (1314–1384/5) appeared in Srinagar, preaching, holding a forty-day retreat (*chilla*), and engaging in conversion. The linkages that form our destiny can entwine strange and mysterious ways. A Kashmiri historian and a member of the Kubrawiyya order introduced into Kashmir, Sayyid Ali in his *Tarikh-i Kashmir* records how before Hamdani's visit, the city maintained at best a weak, faltering connection with the Muslim faith: "At the time of Sayyid 'Ali's visit to Kashmir, there were three to four mosques in the city, but apparently no one would give the call to prayer in these mosques."[1]

Between 1850 and 1860, a richly illuminated Persian manuscript highlighting some of the crafts and professions in Kashmir was produced in Srinagar. The person who commissioned the work remains unknown, but like many such objects produced in colonial India, the manuscript eventually found its way to the British Museum, where it was catalogued as the *Album of Kashmiri Trades*, a name reflecting the colonial desire to understand the lives and practices of the Orient. Another similar manuscript currently housed at Amherst College profiles the people of Kashmir based on their ethnicity and religion—a visual album of ethnography.

In the Album of Kashmiri Trades, there is an intriguing painting depicting the profession of *wazkhani*—sermonizing by Muslim preachers. A young preacher stands on a wooden pulpit (*minbar*), holding a book, surrounded by an attentive congregation of men and women along with a solitary child holding a spinning paper top. The scene is set in the courtyard of Khanqah-i Maula.

## KHANQAH-I MAULA

Immediately below the *khanqah* walls, two Hindu pandits can be seen praying beneath a tree. Overall, the painting captures a serene image of two communities engaging simultaneously in their religious practices within the same precinct, with no signs of conflict. The image bespeaks communal harmony, we believe.

While the subject material may have been dictated by the colonial desire to document, the painting itself was part of an older established tradition, one which we may retrospectively call the *qalam-i Srinagar*, the Srinagar school of painting. After all, it was a flourishing tradition from the seventeenth through the nineteenth centuries, when works composed in Kashmir would be traded in markets down south as well as further west in Kabul and into Iran.

In the Album of Kashmiri Trades, as was usual with such albums, the painting is accompanied by an explanatory text. In the accompanying Persian text, the subject of the painting is introduced as "Illustration of the house and spring of Shri Maha Kali Bhagwati, which Muslims in former times forcibly converted into their shrine". The text then goes on to briefly explain how the Muslims (forcibly) constructed the shrine of Shah Hamdan on the site, which was originally the location of a temple dedicated to the goddess Maha Kali. The illusion of harmony no longer remains, for in the text the artist manages to introduce a narrative of forced possession or, in this case, dispossession. One is tempted to see the album as a product of the colonial enterprise, which seeks to divide communities. Was it so? Or was the artist exercising his agency in introducing a message that seems at odds with the idea of an album showcasing crafts and trade practices?

My earliest memory of the site dates from around 1984 or 1985, when, as a school-going child, I would pass through the *khanqah* compound twice, on my way to and from the bus stop. This brief ten-to-fifteen-minute walk became a daily routine, offering a momentary pause in my school life to say a quick prayer, invariably a wish for the day. As a child, your demands made of the divine keep on changing, and one never compiles a checklist of all the miracles sought and wishes granted. Based solely on my childhood memories, the site appeared to be predominantly Muslim. I don't recall the visual presence of any Hindus, especially Hindu women, who would have been easily distinguishable by their saris or *shalwar kamiz* (trousers and tunic) known as a *kutna*. However, this is just a child's recollection. In reality, Hindus, both men and women, would visit the *khanqah ghat* daily to offer prayers, clean the steps, sprinkle water, and place flowers, mostly marigolds (*gul-i jafar*), which many in the city still refer to as *batey posh* (the Hindu flower) owing to their significance in Hindu *puja* ceremonies. A pandit also used to be in attendance. Despite this, our routines never intersected.

The site, one of the most revered for Kashmiri Muslims, owes its presence to the arrival of the Kubrawiyya shaykh Mir Sayyid Ali Hamdani in the city during the rule of Sultan Qutub al-Din (r. 1373–1389), the brother and successor of Shihab al-Din. Sayyid Ali Hamdani would remain the only transregional head of a Sufi order to arrive in Kashmir, and his visit, even if brief, would lend a level of prestige to the conversion process in Kashmir that was unrivalled. The eighteenth-century Kashmiri historian Khwaja Azam Dedhmari, whose work *Tarikh-i Kashmir* (c. 1159 AH / 1746 CE) remains unsurpassed in its popularity as an account of Muslim rule in Kashmir, writes about the Kubrawiyya shaykh: "In this country, Islam advanced so much that within the heart of its inhabitants, no trace [scent] of infidelity or heresy remained. Due to his auspicious and abundant presence, this country became an unrivalled paradise."[2]

Almost nothing is known about the real reason behind the visit. Most Muslim hagiographers link Ali Hamdani's arrival with the ascendancy of Amir Timur (r. 1370–1405) and his invasion of Iran. In their view, Timur had developed a hostility towards some of the *sayyids* (those claiming descent from the Prophet), but this is not historically proven. Other, mostly oral traditions link the visit to the Sufi practice of travelling, something which was taken up by Ali Hamdani with great enthusiasm. There are also claims that the rulers of Swat were related to Ali Hamdani, and given Kashmir's historical proximity to Swat, the shaykh had simply extended his travels to Kashmir.

For Muslim Kashmir, Sayyid Ali is not only the saint who endowed the land with *din* (religion) but also one who introduced *kasab* (craft) into the region. As Jamal Elias observes in *The Throne Carrier of God*, in the popular Kashmiri imagination Ali Hamdani remains the "bringer of religion and Islamic civilization to a benighted land".

As for the claim that his *khanqah* was built on the site of a temple, we first encounter this in a work authored during the second half of the sixteenth century. The author, Sayyid Ali, himself a member of the Kubrawiyya, asserts that the Hindu priest of an unnamed temple engaged in a feat of spiritual contestation with a disciple of Ali Hamdani. Once defeated, the priest realized the truth of Ali Hamdani's message, accepted Islam, and offered the temple site to the Sufi, who then constructed his *khanqah* in its place.

In the nineteenth century, Sayyid Ali's text was taken up by Pir Hasan Shah in his *Tarikh-i Kashmir*. This work remains the last major historical account of Kashmir in Persian and has attained a level of popular acclaim that even eclipses the earlier work of Dedhmari. It is Hasan who links the site to the temple of Maha Kali. In the politics of the twentieth century, within an increasingly polarized city, the earlier Muslim narratives were presented by Hindus as textual proof of past excesses. Though a small minority in the city, the Hindus could claim the site on the basis of the understanding that a Hindu court would support them. In addition, in colonial narratives, the story of past Muslim excesses and despoliation of Hindu sites takes centre stage. So, as a restive Muslim leadership became assertive about their sense of disenfranchisement, the Hindus also started a campaign to assert control over sites in the city that they saw as their lost sacred spaces. These included the Khanqah-i Maula. This and other similar disputes about the ownership of sites that were seen as "contested" in the years leading up to the formation of Independence have been studied in great detail by Mridu Rai in her book *Hindu Rulers, Muslim Subjects*. Earlier, in 1819, when the victorious Sikh army of the Maharaja of Punjab, Ranjit Singh, arrived in Srinagar after defeating the Afghan *subedar* (provincial administrator) at Shopian, the invaders positioned their cannons on the banks facing the *khanqah*, intending to blow it up. The Muslims, formerly from the ruling classes of the land, now virtually disenfranchised, approached a local Hindu, Pandit Birbal Kak, who had allied with the Sikh army, to intervene. This he did successfully. The monument was saved from destruction, though its doors were sealed, like most Muslim religious places in the city.

Historically, the *khanqah*'s construction took place much later, in 798 AH / 1396 CE, when Ali Hamdani's son, Mir Muhammad Hamdani (1372–1450), arrived in the city. The reigning sultan at that time, Sikandar Shah (r. 1389–1413), undertook the construction at the site of an existing stone platform (*sufa*), where Sayyid Ali had preached and prayed. In medieval texts, we occasionally come across references to a *sufa*, which seems to have been a favoured outdoor sitting area for people: it was ubiquitous in the city landscape, usually being outside a *khanqah* or a mosque. Mulla Ahmad Ali, the author of the medieval hagiographical work *Tuhfatul Ahbab*, recorded an event when nobles and *ulema* of the court assembled on a *sufa* outside the palace upon hearing the news of Sultan Hasan Shah's death. Even today, many prominent *khanqahs* in the city possess a stone *sufa*.

As I have argued in my book on Kashmir's Islamic religious architecture, it is Mir Muhammad Hamdani who would actually popularize the Kubrawiyya order in the city and also lay the material foundation of a Persianate culture in Srinagar. The Sufi and the sultan, both young, would form a close bond of respect and a shared religious vision. Muslim historians and hagiographers have hailed the young sultan as a strong votary of Islam, the man who made Kashmir a Muslim land. He would be remembered as a *But-shikan* (iconoclast), who vandalized Hindu temples. In *Corpus of Sarada Inscriptions of Kashmir*, BK Deambi, a Sanskrit scholar, records an epigraph found in the village of Khanmoh (Khonamosa, in Sanskrit): "When four thousand years increased by five hundred and thirty of the Kali [era] had elapsed, there [ruled] in Satisara a king [named] Jayanolabadenaśāha [Zain al-Abidin], the son of the illustrious Sakandra [Sikandar]."[3] The inscription, written by the sculptor Gaggaka, dates the hermitage's foundation to Zain al-Abidin's reign and mentions Puraka, a merchant, as the patron behind the enterprise. Significantly, for a project located in commonplace community patronage, the project's sponsor chose to present Sikandar in a positive light. This may not be the clinching argument to absolve Sikandar of iconoclastic zeal, yet it does indicate the layered nature of history, something contemporary popular history tends to ignore. Nevertheless, there are numerous instances where we can see Muslim religious places appearing at Hindu sites. So, is it possible that the site has a more ancient past, and that a temple was despoiled in its construction? If architecture is a judge, then assuredly no. The entire site is devoid of any architectural detailing that could link it to the tradition of medieval stone temples.

The initial *khanqah* was a small structure comprising a series of individual buildings that were repeatedly rebuilt. Towards the end of the fifteenth century, another Persian Sufi, Mir Shams al-Din Iraki, arrived in the city. As a member of the Nurbakshiyya order which traced their spiritual lineage to Ali Hamdani, Iraki was left unimpressed by the design and the scale of the *khanqah*, which he deemed unfit for meditation. He rebuilt it as a two-storey structure, and this his biographer sees as a major achievement, both spiritually and architecturally. The present monumental structure that exists at the site, showcasing Kashmiri wooden architecture at its best, is a Mughal construction dating to 1733. It was built at a time of waning imperial authority and provincial discontent. The reconstruction was a Kashmiri affair, in which the custodians of the *khanqah* asked the local court to finance the enterprise. So this Mughal recreation remains, unlike anything else that Mughals built in Kashmir during their heyday. From Akbar till the time of Shah Jahan, the Mughals preferred to construct their buildings in the same style and manner that they used in the imperial cities of Delhi, Agra and Lahore. Traditional Kashmiri architecture was too quaint for their liking; they ignored it both in their personal and public architecture. The mosques they built in the city, Masjid-i Nau, Masjid-i Dara and Masjid-i Mulla Akhund, are great expressions of the empire's munificence, yet the aesthetics of these undertakings are devoid of any Kashmiri context.

While the reconstruction of the *khanqah* was a Mughal affair, the ornamentation and decoration of the interior spaces was a long-drawn-out affair that involved both the court and the merchants of the city. Early in his career, one of modern Kashmir's most famous painters, Ghulam Rasul Santosh (d. 1997), worked as a *naqash* at the site, repainting some of the old, damaged artwork dating to the nineteenth century. When William Carpenter, a watercolour artist, arrived in the city in

# KHANQAH-I MAULA

1856, he drew the shrine's exterior and interior. His painting of an *urs* (anniversary celebration of a saint) provides the first glimpse of the building's interior, with the walls draped in costly textiles, including the famed Kashmiri shawl. The shawl as a motif (paisley) also finds its way into the walls and ceiling of the building in fine papier mâché work. The rich interiors of the *khanqah* continue to define the optics of how Muslim sacred spaces should look. The interiors of two major *khanqahs* in the city, Khanqah-i Naqshbandiyya and Astan-i Pir Dastgir Saheb, were modelled on the Khanqah-i Maula. But then Khanqah-i Maula is not only an architectural wonder. The fate and history of the *khanqah*, besides being intertwined with the religious and cultural landscape of Kashmir, is also an integral part of the political tapestry of the land, both in its celebrations and dissensions. In the sacred geography of Muslim Kashmir, the *khanqah* is described as having "attained the position of the second Kaaba in this country".

1. Jhelum riverfront, Fateh Kadal, Srinagar, 1999.
Photo © Sameer Hamdani.

2. Martand Temple (c. 9th century), showcasing Greek influnces on medieval Kashmiri temple architecture, 2019.
Photo © Sameer Hamdani.

3. Hafiz on a Chinese bill, Srinagar, 19th century.
Photo © Oriental Library, Srinagar.

4. Detailing in a 20th century residence showing varied cultural influences, Aali Kadal, Srinagar, 2004. Photo © Sameer Hamdani.

5. A four-story Pandit house, Zaina Kadal, Srinagar, 2019.
Photo © Shoaib Qasba.

6. Queen Maya holds a branch of the Ashoka tree while giving birth to Siddartha (future Buddha), Kashmir, 7th CE, SPS Museum. Photo © Sameer Hamdani.

7. *Dub*, projecting from a early-20th century merchant home, Pather Masjid, Srinagar, 2022. Photo © Sheikh Intekhab Alam.

8. Wooden portico at Alchi, oldest representation of Kashmiri wooden architecture, 2011. Photo © Sameer Hamdani.

9. Khanqah-i Maula, Jhelum riverfront, Srinagar, 1983.
Photo © Prataap Patrose.

10. Khanqah-i Mula from the album *Trades of Kashmir*. Photo © The British Library.

11. Kucha leading to Khanqah-i Maulla, Srinagar, 2024.
Photo © Ta-Ha Mughal.

# 7
# NAU SHAHR

> *In the absence of arts and riches, worship is rude and destitute of showy accessories.*
>
> Anonymous, Dabistan-i Mazhab

IN THE FIFTEENTH CENTURY, a sultan of Kashmir relocated his capital beyond Koh-i Maran, to the north of the existing city. For centuries, the Koh-i Maran hill had served as the physical and visual boundary of Srinagar. However, numerous ancient sites dotted the landscape in and around the hill, particularly to its west and north. The new city was established in an area that closely overlapped with the older city of Pravarapur. Even today, the ruins of Pravarasena's city can be observed in the area, partially buried under newer constructions. The sultan responsible for the new city had usurped the throne, dispossessing and imprisoning his elder brother, Ali Shah. Unlike Ali Shah, the new sultan was a man of vision, great temperament, and an even greater ability to attract the best talents. In posterity, the people of Kashmir would remember him as Bud Shah (The Great King). His regal title was Qutb al-Din Abu al-Mujahid al-Adil al-Sultan Zain al-Abidin Shah (r. 1420–1470), and he would rule Kashmir for half a century, the longest-reigning Muslim ruler of Kashmir.

We don't know the exact date on which the new capital was inaugurated. In medieval texts it became famous as Razidhaen, a corruption of the Sanskrit *rajdahni*, or capital. Towards the end of the eighteenth century, the name Razidhaen was no longer in vogue, and the city no longer existed. Memory of the past was kept alive by the Persianized name of the former capital, Nau

Shahr, the New City. Today, the area survives as a large suburban housing colony and an industrial area set up in the 1980s within a seventeenth-century Mughal *bagh* (garden). Pandit Jonaraja, the Hindu historian at the court of Zain al-Abidin, called the new capital Zainanagari, and wrote that the new city extended three miles north of the Koh-i Maran, comprising lofty stone buildings, colleges and markets.[1] Members of the court were given land in the new capital and encouraged to resettle there. Nevertheless, many were reluctant to leave the old quarters near the Jhelum and move into the new capital.

The heart of Nau Shahr was the royal palace, designed to impress natives and visitors alike by its sheer size. The palace also went by the same name as the capital, Razidhaen. This is how Mirza Haidar Dughlat, the Mughal conqueror who resided in the palace for twelve years, remembers it in his *Tarikh-i Rashidi*. Dughlat was widely travelled and educated, and connected through blood ties to many of Central Asia's current and former royal houses. As a child, he had grown up under the care of his uncle, Emperor Babur (r. 1526–1530). A connoisseur himself, Dughlat was no admirer of Kashmiris, yet he is very measured in his estimate of the royal palace at Nau Shahr: "It has twelve stories, some of which contain fifty rooms, halls, and corridors. The whole of this lofty structure is built of wood."[2] Dughlat then goes on to compare the architectural pretensions of the Razidhaen with similar royal sites located in Tabriz, Herat and Samarkand, naming each of the principal palaces in these cities. In comparison with these, he argues: "[the Razidhaen] is more lofty and contains more rooms than any of these, yet it has not their elegance and style. It is, nevertheless, a more wonderful structure."[3]

The palace, like much of Nau Shahr, was lost to arson and looting. Still, the vision of a massive structure, with fifty rooms on each floor, and each room spacious enough to accommodate five hundred guests, has continued to preoccupy the imagination of native historians. This preoccupation with size is something that carries over into our own time. There is an obsession among Kashmiris to build oversized homes, with little consideration for their functional needs and practical requirements. A big house, not a beautiful house, is the only way in which a Kashmiri can convey his wealth. It marks his arrival on the social stage. It is something similar to the McMansion phenomenon, which became widespread in the America of the 1980s. In Srinagar, the oldest house in the city dates back to the second half of the nineteenth century. A few years ago, my cousin dismantled his ancestral house. The house was located at Zadibal, a neighbourhood that coincidentally borders Nau Shahr. It was the house where my mother, her father and her grandfather were born. Based on the construction, I always felt that the house must have been built in the 1870s or maybe even later. During the dismantling, the construction date was found carved on one of the wooden beams supporting the room: 1847. The building had served as the *mahal khana* (women's or sleeping quarters) for the family. Another building used as *diwan khana* (men's quarters) survived for a few more years before it was dismantled.

Despite the loss of this family house, the wider neighbourhood retains many old houses dating back to the nineteenth century, belonging to merchants and traders who made money from the lucrative shawl business. These include the Jalali and the Malik houses, both fine representations of the vernacular architecture of Kashmir. Yet, what marks out these houses for special distinction is their sheer size: their horizontal spread. Across the historical builtscape of Srinagar, the same construction detailing, the same decorative features, and the same embellishment can be seen in many houses, whether they belonged to a shawl merchant, a professional, a courtier or an artisan. This uniformity of architecture is best witnessed on the riverfront, with its continuous line of residences on either side. The homogeneous facades could well serve as a poster for socialist architecture, an architecture that makes no distinction between the rich and the poor.

Meanwhile, at Nau Shahr, the only remains of the former capital that survive comprise a small mosque constructed by Sayyid Muhammad Madani, and an even smaller enclosure that serves as the cemetery of Mulla Kabir, the teacher of Zain al-Abidin. There is also a masonry bridge on the verge of extinction, which once served as an aqueduct for water carried into the city from the Sindh canal. The rest is left to our imagination as we try to map the possible contours of a city that now exists in texts alone.

In terms of its material culture, the court of Zain al-Abidin increasingly moved away from an older Indic cultural space to one rooted in the Persianate. This artistic movement was facilitated as much by the court as by Muslim missionaries—Sufis who arrived in the city. Still, Zain al-Abidin's reign marks no abrupt break from the past. Rather, his was a court of intertwined traditions. His court historians were both Muslim and Hindu, and the languages in which they wrote were Persian and Sanskrit.

# 8

## JAMIA-I SRINAGAR

*The Masjeda was a spacious building, extending on all sides, and was always whitewashed [...] It was within this building that crowds of worshippers used to fall down and rise at prayers, imitating the high waves of Sangaravra. It was here that the Yavanas [foreigners] chanted mantras and looked graceful, like thousand lotuses with humming bees [...] It was here the four minarets looked graceful like the supports of virtue, as if virtue had left his own place and descended to this spot to witness if the people observed the rules of religion. It was here that the sun shone like an umbrella of gold, as if he came hither to listen to the vanities of the world. Such was the great building which towered to the sky and was decorated with wonderful sculptures, and which appeared like a fortress for the preservation of the faith of the mlechchaking [...] It was here that in times of edha and other festivals, the mlechchha people used to gather in crowds and observe the rites of religion with devotion.*

Pandit Shrivara, *Rajatarangini*

IN THESE POIGNANT SANSKRIT verses, Pandit Shrivara, the fifteenth-century historian and confidant of three Muslim sultans of Kashmir, describes the Jamia of Srinagar. The verses do justice to a physical landscape that continues to fascinate. Even in its English translation, the text creates dramatic imagery out of the mosque's architecture and the physical act of worshipping. Shrivara's description was written in the aftermath of a fire that burned the mosque and entire neighbourhoods in the city. The mosque would be rebuilt again, only to be burned twice more before its final reconstruction during the reign of the Mughal emperor Aurangzeb (r. 1658–1707).

Archival images from the early twentieth century show traces of white plaster on the mosque facade, but this no longer survives. Between 1907 and 1930, the Archaeological Survey of India extensively repaired the mosque under the supervision of its director, Sir John Marshall. In the restoration, the brick masonry was left exposed. This decision may have been influenced by a paucity of funds or else by creeping modern sensibilities that preferred to keep the extensive masonry arcade exposed.

Today, the building is markedly devoid of any decorative enrichment on the surfaces; the walls are plain and unadorned. Still, the interiors represent a maze of wooden columns, almost like a forest, conveying the sense of awe that we find in Shrivara's verses. But that is just about it. Somehow, the building seems too austere, simply plain. However, this was not the case during Shrivara's time or even later when Kashmir was incorporated into the Mughal Empire. In his autobiography, the fourth Mughal emperor, Jahangir, a great aesthete himself, described the mosque as a "fine building" with "very fine painted and decorated pillars".[1]

Earlier native Kashmiri historians had described the magnificence of the mosque. The seventeenth-century author of *Baharistan-i Shahi* writes about the building with a sense of pride and wonderment, describing the Jamia of Srinagar as a unique structure: "Throughout the lands of Hind and Sindh and the climes of Iran and Turan, one cannot come across a mosque of such grandeur and magnificence, though of course such grand mosques do exist in the lands of Egypt and Syria."[2]

The Jamia Srinagar is a unique exemplar of a new language of design—a *tarah*—marking the successful coming together of a visual grammar linked to Kashmir's pre-Islamic past and to ideas of aesthetics and planning that originated in the Persianate lands in Iran and Central Asia. It remains the most successful monument commissioned and realized during the rule of the sultans of Kashmir. The basic plan of the mosque is Persian in its inspiration, borrowing from what is now known as the Iranian mosque plan, or the four-*iwan* courtyard plan.

The four-*iwan* plan was introduced in the Islamic world in the eleventh century and is associated with the Seljuks. It became the most prominent and widespread form of the Jamia mosque in Iran, and remained an essential feature of what has been defined as the Iranian mosque, spreading from the land of its origin and becoming an accepted model in areas as far-flung and diverse as Transoxiana and India. The first four-*iwan* mosque in India, the Begampur Friday mosque, had been constructed by the Tughlaqs at their capital Jahanpanah (Delhi) in 1343, virtually around the same time that the Shahmiri sultanate was being established in Kashmir. The adoption of this plan in Kashmir, nearly a century after the establishment of Muslim rule in the region, was accompanied by a steady arrival of Persian missionaries and artisans.

Persian sources attribute the mosque's construction to the Kubrawiyya Sufi, Mir Muhammad Hamdani. Hamdani shared a close friendship with the young sultan, Sikandar Shah, serving as his religious guide while the sultan acted as a generous benefactor. The sultan commissioned the construction, with the Sufi overseeing the project. After the masonry walls repeatedly collapsed, two of Hamdani's associates, both natives of Iran, supervised the work on site. Construction of the mosque was completed in 840 AH / 1402 CE.

What helps to place the mosque in a Kashmiri context is the form of the roof and the spire, which replace the dome, vault and minaret of the Iranian landscape. The sloping roof of the mosque, once covered with birch bark and earth and planted with black tulips and irises, is supported by a system of wooden columns and beams. The origin of this construction could be native, as we see similar examples in Alchi temples, though on a much smaller scale. Or it could be inspired by similar examples further west, like the Jamia-i Khiva, a tenth-century mosque in modern Uzbekistan with a similar layout of wooden columns and beams. Unlike the support system of the ceiling, the spire is conspicuously Kashmiri. Pyramidal with smaller side gables at the base, they replicate the form and detailing that we see in a medieval stone temple. The gilded finial, *dastar,* in the local vernacular, is again built in the image of the *kalash* (parasol) that we find in both Buddhist and Hindu architecture.

The traditional approach to the mosque was on its west side, through a maze of narrow alleys and meandering streets leading to the Mar canal. To its east, sloping towards the Koh-i Maran, lay a vast open maidan (town square) which was gradually transformed into two separate cemeteries, Mazar-i Kalan and Malkah.

During the rule of Emperor Jahangir, the mosque was destroyed by fire. This was not the first time the building had caught fire, nor was it to be the last. The mosque's reconstruction was taken up by Malik Haidar, a Kashmiri noble who enjoyed the court's favours, especially those of Empress Nur Jahan. Haidar had rescued Nur Jahan in faraway Bengal after her first husband was killed by Mughal soldiers at the instigation of Jahangir. This event, which happened before Nur Jahan's marriage to Jahangir, was remembered by the royal couple. Moreover, Haidar was an accomplished engineer, the perfect choice for the reconstruction, which was completed in 1620. The emperor had the chronogram, composed by Haidar, carved at the royal workshop in Agra and then transported to Srinagar for installation a year after work at the site had finished. The inscription highlights earlier repairs to the mosque, and seeks to publicize the Mughal reconstruction as part of a historic scheme of pious patronage linked with Srinagar's principal mosque. A textual narrative is constructed that presents Jahangir as the legitimate heir to the rulership of Kashmir. The epigraph reads:

> The first congregational mosque was built by the Iskandar Shah II,
> and then it burned by divine destiny.
> Another time Hasan Shah, he who was of his pure progeny,
> became the builder of this mosque, also with divine assistance
> But on two sides nine pillars adorned its nine roofs.
> By Ibrahim son of Ahmad Magre it became right so you may know.
> Of the Hegira nine hundred and nine [1503 CE] it was when, during the reign of Muhammad Shah,
> this paradisiacal place became the ornament of the Muslim religion.
> On the date one thousand and twenty-nine [1619 CE] of the Hegira of the Lord [of all creatures]
> on the holiday of fasting it burned a second time.
> During Jahangir's reign, Malik Haidar *Rai's-ul Mulk* laid the foundation
> again on the day of the feast of the sacrifice.
> When he sought the date of its construction a voice of inspiration said:
> He laid its foundation again at the time of the feast of the sacrifice [1029 AH / 1620 CE]
> Hasan Sultan Malik Najji repaired the Kashmir mosque
> Under his supervision Malik Haidar *Rai's-ul Mulk* completed it.
> Finished in Agra in the year '31
> Muhammad Murad [?calligrapher]

Made [stone carved] by Hari Ram[3]

Located prominently on the main southern entrance gateway to the mosque, the inscription also records the names of the Kashmiri master calligrapher Muhammad Murad and the Hindu stone carver Hari Ram. This is the only known case from the Mughal period in which the name of a non-Muslim is prominently displayed on the walls of a Jamia masjid.

# 9

# DUMATH

IN HIS *MUQADDIMAH* (INTRODUCTION), the Arab historian Ibn Khaldun describes how a monument not only serves as the enduring legacy of a ruling dynasty but is also commensurate with its power and acclaim. In its architectural design and achievement, a monument represents the "strengths and the weakness" not of a particular ruler alone but of an entire dynasty responsible for its construction and upkeep. So it was that Sultan Habib Shah (r. 1557–1561) of the House of Shahmir, on visiting Mazar-i Salatin, the royal cemetery of the sultans of Kashmir, decided to expand it. The act was dictated as much by filial piety as pragmatism. The chronogram for the new extension, carved on a stone gateway, makes this quite obvious:

> Sultan Habib made a stop at the graveyard of his ancestors
> He surveyed it and said: soon this place of the Kings will be straightened.
> He expanded it, and added a porch and a door on its side
> So no King may be deprived of attaining a place therein.
> Of its reconstruction, I heard from the Angel.
> The year of its founding is: the second graveyard of Sultan Habib[1]

Unfortunately for the young sultan, this limited architectural intervention proved his only claim to greatness. In 1561, he was deposed by his battle-hardened uncle Ghazi Shah Chak (r. 1561–1563), and a new, short-lived dynasty, the Chaks (r. 1561–1589), came to rule Kashmir. Today, the gateway no longer exists, and the damaged stone inscription lies abandoned outside the royal cemetery. A temporary tea stall stands next to it; passersby seem oblivious to its history. The fate of this epigraph mirrors that of the young sultan, discarded and forgotten.

However, something more substantial did survive at the site. Next to the royal cemetery stands the only Muslim mausoleum built in Kashmir during the rule of the sultans. The monument, uniquely situated in a city of shrines honouring pious, saintly men, is dedicated to the memory of a woman—a queen. Dumath, as the mausoleum is known in Kashmiri on account of its shape, was constructed by Sultan Zain al-Abidin in memory of his mother. The monument is part of the larger precinct surrounding Mazar-i Salatin. The approach to the site is from a narrow street lined with copper shops leading to a stone gateway that is partially hidden. The gateway still bears traces of its original iconography and was certainly a Hindu site. Much of the material from the original site, *spolia*, has been used in the plinth of both the Dumath and the walls of the open enclosure that serves as the burial place for the sultans of the Shahmiri dynasty. Unlike the mausoleum, the royal enclosure is extremely plain, the monotony of the wall broken by a series of arched niches.

The architecture of the mausoleum seems far removed from what we know of the traditional Kashmiri way of building. The design of the Dumath reveals Timurid influences, which were gradually making their way into the court of the Kashmiri sultans. Arched entrance portals, domes supported on high drums, and a facade decoration in mosaic tiles are essential elements of Timurid architecture. We can observe these at Dumath too, though on a much-reduced scale. The combination of the brick masonry and turquoise-blue glazed tile work that we see on the facade can also be observed in the building at the Shah-i Zinda necropolis in Samarkand. In local traditions, the design of the Dumath is said to have been inspired by the Gur-i Amir, the Timurid mausoleum built by Amir Timur at Samarkand. Yet the shape of the central dome, surrounded by four cupolas, is unlike anything observable in Timurid architecture. It has a distinctly Byzantine appearance. So what could be the inspiration behind the dome? In 1453, when Zain al-Abidin was at the peak of his rule, Constantinople fell to the Ottoman Army. Most historians believe that many people in the former Byzantine Empire fled westwards to continental Europe. Was there also a movement to the east, one that made it to Kashmir as well? We have no way of knowing, but the design of the Dumath, especially the dome, does raise the possibility.

# 10

## A MUGHAL EMPEROR IN THE CITY

> *sukhandarvasf-i Kashmīr astbījā*
> *zabānīnjā bi-band u dīdabugshā*
>
> Poetry describing Kashmir is out of place;
> shut your mouth here and open your eyes.
>
> Ali Saidi, an Iranian poet<br>at the Mughal court[1]

IN THE YEAR 1073 of the Hijra (1664 CE), a French physician at the Mughal court, François Bernier, slipped into Kashmir, travelling with Nawab Danishmand Khan, a Mughal noble of Iranian descent.[2] The nawab was part of a limited entourage, lucky enough to receive an imperial pass to travel to Kashmir along with the emperor. After his accession, this was to be the first visit of Muhi al-Din Muhammad Aurangzeb Alamgir (1658–1707), the sixth Mughal emperor, to the northernmost *subah* (province) of his empire. Earlier, as the imperial party left Shahjahanabad (Delhi), the streets of the capital were rife with rumours about the possible reasons for this sudden departure. Some whispered that the journey was a ruse: the real destination was in the west, to recapture the fort of Kandahar from the Persians. Other more ominous voices spoke about the emperor's ill health and claimed the trip had been advised by royal physicians for the convalescing ruler. The Venetian Niccolao Manucci, who was also in residence at Shahjahanabad (Delhi), credits the emperor's favourite sister, Roshan Ara Begum (d. 1671), with the journey. The march to Kashmir was her idea, Manucci believed, being intended to create a grand spectacle along the route and parade her new status as the leading lady of the imperial harem.

So, even with limitations on who could travel, the imperial party was nevertheless a large one, befitting the prestige of the Great Moghul and Roshan Ara's desire to impress. In his letters the Frenchman Bernier complained about the progress of the journey. Slowly, the imperial party marched along the Mughal Road, from Delhi to Lahore, and then across the formidable Pir Panjal mountain range into Kashmir. The *subedar* of Kashmir had stationed fifteen thousand porters at the frontier post of Bhimber to await the arrival of the imperial party. At Bhimber, it was hot and suffocating, and Bernier repeatedly grumbled about the place. A noble of the court, along with guards, was stationed at the mountain pass leading into Kashmir, and all those who had failed to obtain an imperial permit were turned back. Nobles, as well as peripatetic merchants and traders seeking to make a quick profit from the opportunity that the emperor's visit offered, found their path closed by the emperor's guards.

Although they left Shahjahanabad in December, it was only on 28 May that the imperial party arrived in Srinagar, the City of Kashmir. The descent into the city must have presented a visual extravaganza: in those days it commonly took the form of a riverine procession. On reaching Baramulla, the imperial party would have embarked and joined a procession of boats on the river Jhelum. Earlier, during the time of Emperor Akbar (r. 1556–1605), several newly designed boats were introduced in Kashmir, including double-storeyed boats with prows carved in the likeness of mythical creatures. Curiously, Akbar's son and successor, Jahangir, writes about a boat of "Kashmiri design" with a silver seat presented to him by Shah Jahan. Even as a young prince, the emperor who would go on to erect the Taj Mahal had a fine appreciation of all things beautiful. Inheriting the Mughal tradition of building with red sandstone, he left them clad in marble like the Roman emperor Augustus. Moreover, Shah Jahan had an uncanny ability to pick seemingly commonplace objects and motifs and transform them into something exquisite, such as the *bangla* roof with its drop-down corners, which from a humble origin in a Bengali hut became a symbol of royalty in its new avatar as a marble *jarokha* (window). So it was perhaps with the quaint Kashmiri boat. The numerous *shikaras* that are eagerly sought by visitors for a boat ride on the Dal Lake are of modern design. The design was inspired by the punt that colonial officials visiting the valley in the nineteenth and twentieth centuries would use to hunt (*shikar*).

The author of *Padshahnama*, the official history of the reign of Shah Jahan, recounts the imperial fascination with the waterways of the city during his rule: "Another feature of Srinagar is that walking around and sightseeing are undertaken in boats. A branch of the Dal water merges into the Jhelum. Wealthy, respectable people, especially court nobles (*shahi mansabdars*) whose *havelis* [townhouses] are located on this river and the lake, travel in boats along this channel to reach the *durbar* [court]. Thousands of colourful, painted and decorated boats move back and forth on the Jhelum River and Dal Lake. They are covered with rich curtains [...]."[3]

From its origin at Verinag, the location of a sixteenth-century Mughal pavilion and garden, the Jhelum slowly meanders through the valley of Kashmir in a southerly direction. Barring occasional floods, the river's flow is unhurried, giving enough time for travellers to gaze at the not-so-distant snow-capped mountains, across vistas of open green fields and willow-lined banks. Moving against the flow, the imperial procession would have made its way through the heart of the city, lined as it was on either bank with high stone embankment walls supporting "houses of two, three, and four stories and roofs covered with mud".[4] In 1853, the British watercolour artist William Carpenter made his way into Kashmir, where he would paint numerous scenes both during this and subsequent visits in 1854 and 1855. Two of the watercolours are of the riverfront and convey visually very much like what was depicted in the Mughal texts. Beyond the city limits, the imperial procession would have proceeded into a side channel, Tsunth Kul (Apple Canal), which links the Jhelum to the famed Dal Lake, the latter lined with numerous gardens belonging to the royal family and privileged *amirs* at the court. But before visiting the gardens, the procession would have first made an official landing at Naagar Nagar.

In the city, the final destination of the emperor was the walled encampment of Naagar Nagar established around the hillock of Koh-i Maran. This was a city within the city, reserved for the Mughals. On the south and west, a vast public cemetery, Malkah, established during the fifteenth and sixteenth centuries by Sufis belonging to the Kubrawiyya order, separated Naagar Nagar from the native quarters of the city. And on its east side, the hillock gently sloped into the blue waters of Sadrakhun Lake, the Nigeen of the Mughals. On this side of the hill were to be found the royal palace, the *havelis* of the *umra* (nobles), and the gardens belonging to members of the royal family and leading nobles of the court. There was also an atelier with painted depictions of the various stages of travel from Lahore to Kashmir, commissioned by Aurangzeb's grandfather, Emperor Jahangir (r. 1605–1627). The Mughals were good at committing royal events to illustration, in small-size paintings that were then pasted in albums (*muraqqa*), often referred to misleadingly as Mughal miniatures. In the late eighteenth and early part of the nineteenth century, when Mughal rule was but a distant memory, Srinagar gained a reputation as a centre of manuscript production and book-binding. While most of this fame was based on lavishly decorated, illuminated codices of the Quran, artists in the city also focused on copying poetical works of Persian masters such as Hafiz Shirazi (d. 1390), and Shaykh Saadi (d. 1291). These mass-produced poetical compositions were aimed at a non-local audience, much like the curios of today's tourist market. The paintings, though interesting and historical, display none of the magnificence and verve of earlier Mughal works.

Unfortunately, we have no visual or even textual record of Aurangzeb's arrival in Srinagar. In general, from what little details have survived in Bernier's account and the semi-official history of the emperor's reign, *Maasir-i-Alamgiri*, written by the *munshi* Saqi Mustad Khan, the visit seems to have been a pretty drab, business-like affair. It certainly had none of the splendour and exuberance that marked Jahangir's or even Shah Jahan's visits to the valley. It seems that early in his reign, the emperor, who would gain a reputation for his puritanical outlook, had little interest in partying or flaunting his worldliness. Any lavish party-making would have taken place behind the curtains of *harem* privacy, presided over by Roshan Ara Begum. If Manucci's account is to be believed, Roshan Ara's life was free from any restraint and was given over to hedonistic excess. Maybe this is simple Orientalism, which we encounter in both Manucci and Bernier.

Aurangzeb did, however, celebrate his birthday in Srinagar, though the event evoked no lasting memory for the historians to record. Earlier, on a similar occasion during Shah Jahan's reign, while the *durbar* was engaged in festivities, the *subedar*, Zafar Khan Ahsan, used the opportunity to ask for the remission of taxes and levies that had been imposed on Kashmiris. This the emperor did, issuing a royal *farman* (decree). For greater publicity, the *farman* was inscribed on stone and placed on the main door of the city mosque, the Jamia Masjid.

The emperor's arrival also coincided with early summer. Both wild and cultivated flowers would have been in full bloom in fields and *baghs* (gardens), including the rose, poppy and iris. Both rose and poppy remain much-favoured motifs in Mughal art. During his visits to Kashmir, Jahangir had asked his master painter, the *Nadir-al Asr* (Unequalled of the Age), Ustad Mansur (d. 1624), to paint the flowers in the valley. Of the hundred flowers painted by him, only a single one of a *gul-i lala* (red tulip) survives.[5] Ever since Empress Nur Jahan (d. 1645) introduced them in her garden, the cultivation of roses had spread across the *baghs* of Kashmir. One of the gardens, a favourite of Jahangir, Bagh-i Nurafza, was situated in the palace gardens at Naagar Nagar. This *bagh* had a special place for the imperial family, connected as it was with the memory of Emperor Akbar, who annexed Kashmir in 1586. His son, Jahangir, who renovated the buildings within this garden, fondly recalls in his memoirs: "On the palace grounds is a small garden with a small building in the middle, and there my exalted father used often to sit [....] M'tamad Khan had the buildings reconstructed and decorated by master painters whose work would make the painters of China jealous. I named the garden Nurafza."[6] Ironically, fourteen years later, Aurangzeb would issue a *farman* banning the cultivation of roses in all of his gardens except those in two palaces of Shahjahanabad. Whether the gardeners in Kashmir also implemented this imperial decree, we simply don't know.

Today, except for a few scattered mounds of masonry, nothing remains of the palace or the pavilion within the garden. The garden survives as a public park, Badamwari (The Abode of Almond Trees), renovated almost a decade ago by Kashmir's leading financial institution, the Jammu & Kashmir Bank. This is a case of seventeenth-century imperial prestige silently making way for a financial powerhouse of our times! Come spring, many people from the older parts of the city visit the park to witness the blossoms on the almond trees, some nearly a century old. Another imperial garden, a favourite of Nur Jahan, Bagh-i Bahr Ara (Garden of the Ocean Adorner), was situated on the opposite bank and dropped down to the turquoise-blue waters of Nigeen Lake in two majestic terraces. The garden faced the royal viewing window (*jarokha darshan*) of the palace. In 1891, given its distance from the habitable parts of the city, the site was converted into a sanatorium for persons affected by leprosy. Doctors from the Christian Missionary Society, who managed it, also gave it the colonial name by which it is known today, the Leper Colony. A small group of former patients and their families live here, functioning as a community of social outcasts. Earlier, in the 1980s, many of the inhabitants would work on construction sites as the area became urbanized, providing cheap labour. Given the stigma associated with the disease, they used their own kitchen, as sharing food and utensils was seen as taboo.

But Naagar Nagar, despite its splendour, was also problematic. The landscape of Kashmir, celebrated by Mughal emperors, nobles and poets alike, was littered with monuments linked to the memory of Aurangzeb's ill-fated rival and elder brother, Dara Shikoh (d. 1659). As heir presumptive to the Mughal throne, Dara, who lost both the throne and his life in a war of succession, had a genuine attachment to the land, which Aurangzeb never attempted to recreate. This was particularly evident in Naagar Nagar. In the seventeenth century, the main southern face of the hillock was dominated by a vast religious complex, owing its patronage to Dara and his sister Jahanara Begum (d. 1681). This comprised two mosques, located within a terraced garden, along with a *sarai* (rest house). Even today, the ruins of this site command a fine view of the city. The main mosque was commissioned by Jahanara Begum for the Qadri Sufi Akhund Mulla Shah Badakshi and was still incomplete when Aurangzeb seized the throne. It remains so even today, with half-finished verses by Kalim Kashani in bold *thuluth* script inscribed on the outer western wall.

## CITY OF KASHMIR

Earlier, on his arrival in Kashmir, Mulla Shah had run into trouble with a group of Kashmiri *ulema*, who were convinced that he had blasphemed the Prophet in his poetry. They issued a *mazhar* (legal pronouncement) for Badakshi's execution as a heretic. The Mughal *subedar* dithered, but the *ulema* were relentless in pressing the issue. Fearing a riot, he gave in, and the death decree was issued, to be confirmed by the emperor in Delhi. Dara intervened with his father and had the decree rescinded. The prince and his favourite sibling, Jahanara, then became part of the inner circle of Badakshi's disciples, resulting in significant architectural activity in Kashmir, both at Naagar Nagar and in the countryside. Badakshi also wrote a *masnavi*, entitled (in translation) *Palaces, Gardens and the Buildings of the Heart-Pleasing Kashmir*. In his *masnavi* he described some of the structures at Naagar Nagar; these include the mosque, his own house with its *chinikhana* (room for the display of Chinese porcelain), and warm water for ablutions in the mirrored *hammam* (hot bath); the *haveli* of Dara; and some of the prominent gardens in Srinagar belonging to the imperial family as well as leading nobles at the court. Dara himself, in *Sakinat-ul-Awliya*, his treatise on Sufism, described the mosque–*khanqah* complex as "located in the middle of the Kashmir Fort on Koh-Hari Hill, which is a very pleasant place with a view of the city below".[7]

In the seventeenth century, composing lengthy panegyric odes celebrating the "paradise-like" landscape of Kashmir developed into something of a fashion at the Mughal court. Additionally, Kashmir served as a perfect canvas for the extravagant display of Mughal patronage, the size and scale of which was something Kashmir had not seen before, at least in recent memory. The nearest parallel was the rule of the fifteenth-century native sultan Zain al-Abidin, but even his endeavours paled in the face of the scale of Mughal enterprise. And what the Mughals built, their poets sought to celebrate. Soon, native Kashmiri poets who had also taken to composing poetry in Persian, as opposed to their vernacular Kashmiri, sought to impress their audiences with this unbounded munificence of the empire. In a desire to access royal favour and patronage, they competed with the court poets in their carefully crafted verses full of literary conceits associated with *tarz-i tazza* (the new style) or the *sabak-hindi* (Indian school).

Shah Jahan's poet laureate, Abu Talib Kalim Kashani (d. 1651), composed one such poem, with a description of palaces and gardens built by the Mughals. So did Hajji Muhammad Jan Qudsi. In later centuries, the fascination with the Mughal imagining of Kashmir as a paradise would resonate with natives as well as with visitors to Kashmir. An extremely popular though modest verse at best, which may or may not have been written by great Persian masters such as Amir Khusrau (d.1325) or Urfi Shirazi (d. 1591), is frequently appropriated for the Bagh-i Faiz Baksh (Shalimar Garden) at Srinagar:

> Agar firdaus bar ru-ye zaminast
> Haminast-o haminast-o haminast
>
> [If there is heaven on earth
> It is this, it is this, it is this!]

After Dara's execution, Badakshi, as could have been expected, fell out of favour with the new emperor. Almost immediately, Aurangzeb had him recalled to Lahore, where the shaykh was to spend the rest of his life in the heat of the plains, never to return to Kashmir or his *khanqah*. With his removal, the branch of the Qadri order established by Badakshi in Kashmir ceased to exist. And, with Roshan Ara in charge of the *harem*, Jahanara, who had served in the same capacity for many years during the reign of Shah Jahan, lapsed into a diminished public role. The official Mughal records do not mention if she ever visited Kashmir again. In the absence of the three—Dara, Jahanara and Badakshi—the exquisite mosque complex at Naagar Nagar slowly crumbled, first into disuse and then into a state of decay.

On a lower terrace, to the east of the mosque commissioned by Jahanara, we find a more modest structure, the *hammam* (bathhouse) and mosque of Dara. Today these two buildings are the only remnants of the vast architectural proclivity of three generations of Mughal emperors in Naagar Nagar, starting with Emperor Akbar. After taking Kashmir in 1586, Akbar commissioned the construction of a rampart wall (*kalaye*, in Kashmiri) around Koh-i Maran. Aurangzeb did not commission any new structure or garden himself. The *haveli* of Dara, which receives detailed mention in Badakshi's *masnavi*, reverted to his younger brother, the emperor. The *haveli* adjoined the mosque that Dara had built.

In the end, Aurangzeb's journey was to prove a disappointment for the emperor, and he never returned. It was also to be the last time a Mughal emperor would travel to Kashmir. Nevertheless, he would stay here for six months, ample time for Bernier to explore the "Paradise of the Indies". It is Bernier, rather than official Mughal historians, who serves as the key source for the visit. For the Mughals, Kashmir was an unrivalled terrestrial paradise, a *jannat-i benazir*, which poets in the court were expected to celebrate. As often happens, this tradition of celebrating the natural beauty of Kashmir was taken up by newcomers at the royal court, desirous of winning the emperor's approval through gracefully crafted verses. Bernier certainly matched the Persian poets in his praise of Kashmir. For future European visitors to Kashmir, Bernier set the bar for expectations of a beautiful land and an equally beautiful people:

> The capital of Kachmire bears the same name as the kingdom. It is without walls and is not less than three quarters of a league in length, and half a league in breadth [...] In the

town there are two wooden bridges thrown over the river; and the houses, although for the most part of wood, are well built and consist of two or three storeys [...] Most of the houses along the banks of the river have little gardens, which produce a very pretty effect, especially in the spring and summer, when many parties of pleasure take place on the water. Indeed most houses in the city have also their gardens; and many have a canal, on which the owner keeps a pleasure-boat, thus communicating with the lake.[8]

Overall, when reading Mughal accounts, both official historical texts and poetical works, one gets an impression of the city, and Kashmir at large, as a content land, full of beautiful things. The focus in these texts is more on the land, or rather the beauty of the land, and how it has been embellished by the Mughals through their lavish patronage of architecture. Kashmir is magnificent, not only because God made it so but because of the richness and extravagance of Mughal munificence.

Away from the pomp of the walled Mughal enclosure stood the real city of Kashmir, Srinagar. The old city, much like the people of Kashmir, was somewhere in the background, nearby but not near enough. At times, Mughal writings present misogynistic and chauvinistic caricatures of the city and its people. Jahangir, who was besotted with the land, was quite dismissive of the people, the "animal-like Kashmiris". Shah Jahan's historian, Muhammad Salih Kambo, similarly glorified the Mughal conquest of Kashmir as an enterprise to civilize the natives: "When the land came under Akbar, it [Kashmir] achieved new heights [...] People of this land were absolutely unsophisticated and uncivilized drunkards [before Mughal conquest], but became good mannered and cultured [...] Slowly they [Kashmiris] became knowledgeable and [consequently] well versed in the etiquette of assembly [adāb-i Majlis]."[9]

# 11

MAZAR-I SHOURA

IN THE EARLY TWENTIETH century, while lamenting the loss of historic sites in Srinagar, two Kashmiri historians, Munshi Muhammad Din Fauq and Mufti Muhammad Shah Saadat, commented how unique it was that the city possessed a cemetery dedicated to poets: the Mazar-i Shoura. Both Fauq and Saadat were prolific writers who composed a range of texts, including guidebooks, hagiographies and popular histories on everything connected with Kashmir. Mufti Saadat belonged to a family of religious scholars, the Muftis of Wazipora, a *mohalla* in the old city, more famous today as the centre of Kashmiri cuisine (*wazwan*) than any claim to religious scholarship. Fauq, on the other hand, was part of the Kashmiri diaspora based in Lahore, Punjab. His ancestors had migrated to Lahore, along with countless other Kashmiri families.

This migration was not a single event but occurred in cycles during the second and third quarters of the nineteenth century. The movement to Punjab was necessitated by famine and an oppressive taxation system in Kashmir, as a result of which countless people starved to death. To survive, many looked to escape from their homeland through hidden passes and routes, some bribing and some stealing their way into Punjab. On their arrival, these Kashmiri migrants started a new life, working as menial labourers on farms and construction sites in Punjab. Some who had migrated from Srinagar belonged to the artisan class, mostly shawl weavers. In the city and towns of Punjab, they began a new life, toiling in workshops as weavers, embroiderers and darners of shawls. Those born into more comfortable circumstances chose to serve in the professions, working as scribes, secretaries and teachers or setting up their own business ventures. Many of those Kashmiris educated in Lahore maintained a healthy interest in the affairs of Kashmir and its past, some revisiting their homeland.

In their attempt to map the past, both Fauq and Saadat conducted an extensive survey of Kashmir, searching for material or literary evidence that could help document their work. As expected, both were also heavily focused on the Muslim past of the city and of Kashmir. In many instances, Saadat repeats arguments made earlier by Fauq in his writings; this is true, for example, in the description of monuments and cultural sites. For Fauq's readers, the *mazar* served as a strong reminder of how the city of Srinagar had functioned as the last major northern outpost linked to the Persianate culture in South Asia. The *mazar* was not just the marker of a funerary landscape but symbolized a cultural high point linked with Srinagar's past. It was testimony to the mobility of ideas, people and intellectual capacities, all drawn into the city, of which both Fauq and Saadat were acutely aware.

At the time the two historians were busy trying to rehabilitate Mazar-i Shoura in people's consciousness, the site had already been vandalized and despoiled of much of its historical material, especially its tombstones. Within Kashmiri Muslim society, there has always been a certain amount of reverence for the dead. You don't steal from the dead, even though the Kashmiri language retains a saying that warns against those who try to commit this heinous act. But this is more symbolic than literal: the city never had a tradition of people bold enough to be tomb raiders. Even today, when faith and traditions have been rationalized under the influence of modernity, people tend to approach a *mazar* with a measure of hesitancy. A *mazar* is not a site to be dreaded, but it is certainly one that is often avoided.

Additionally, Mazar-i Shoura stood in isolation from the city for most of its history. Located on the foothills of the Takht-i

Sulaiman, the cemetery commands a fine view of the city. In the past, accessing the site would have been time-consuming, especially for those visiting from the city. The only habitation near the *mazar* was a small hamlet called Drugjan. At the time when our historians wrote about the *mazar*, Drugjan was most likely just a handful of houses. So what happened to the *mazar*? No one really knows. Only one tombstone survives, inscribed with a Persian chronogram in a fine *nastaliq* script, marking the death of the poet Salim Tehrani (d. 1647). It lies forgotten in the back storage rooms of the city museum, and hardly anyone is aware of its existence. Even Fauq, who in his writings claims to have seen some of the graves in the cemetery, is silent about it. The writing on Salim's tombstone seems quite ordinary; it certainly lacks any poetical flourish and simply reads:

> He is the Forgiving.
> The sage and the scholar
> In need of the Lord's generous forgiveness
> Muhammad son of Salih—Muhammad Salim Tehrani
> In the year 1047
> of the Hijrah of the Prophet.[1]

Salim had arrived at the court of Shah Jahan from Iran, like many others before him. In a verse that may or may not be his, the attraction the Mughal court had for many literati like himself is made clear:

> The means of acquiring perfection do not exist in Iran.
> Henna did not acquire color till it came to Indian.[2]

At the Mughal court, to gain imperial patronage, you had to manoeuvre your way through a complex web of networks, talents and bitter rivalries. It always helped if your fame preceded you, but one could not rest on one's past laurels and ease one's way into fortune. Unfortunately for Salim, his conceit or perhaps procrastination nearly proved his downfall. The emperor asked the poet to write a *masnavi* or ode in praise of Kashmir and the numerous *baghs* he had developed in the city and the countryside. Many had already done this; some had been commissioned. Salim thought of a stratagem to work his way around the task. He had already written a lengthy *masnavi* praising his native Khurasan in Iran. So he simply replaced Khurasan with Kashmir. The literary tropes that celebrated Khurasan as a paradise worked equally well for Kashmir. The ode was presented to Shah Jahan, but before the poet could hope for a reward, his envious rivals used the occasion to present Salim to the emperor as a plagiarist of his own words!

Of the great Persian poets buried in the *mazar* we have names such as Shah Aboul Fateh (d. 1587) and Kalim Kashani (d. 1651). In 1632, Shah Jahan bestowed the title of *malik-o shoura* (poet laureate) on Kalim and allowed him to take up residence in Srinagar to write a *masnavi* on the reign and achievements of the emperor. Kalim's death left the work, the *Shah Nama*, incomplete. A contemporary of Kalim, the celebrated poet Hajji Muhammad Jan Qudsi (d. 1646), who was also a frequent visitor to Kashmir, composed a lengthy *masnavi*, as did most other poets of his time, on the various stages of the journey to Kashmir. Qudsi was long said to have been buried in the *mazar*, though most historians now agree that his burial occurred in Lahore. Still, of the numerous Persian poets who arrived in Srinagar, Qudsi alone retains some degree of popular remembrance. This is solely based on his religious poetry, poems in praise of the Prophet Muhammad, one of which is sometimes recited in private assemblies hosted in honour of the Prophet (*mehfil-i mawlud*). Another Iranian contemporary of Kalim, Tughra Mashadi (d. 1667/8), who also wrote a *masnavi* about the wonders of Kashmir, *Risalah-i Firdausiya* (The Paradisal Epistle), spent his last years in Srinagar, his writing being enabled by heavy doses of opium. On his death, he was buried in a plot next to Kalim. Unlike Kalim, whose generous nature made everyone befriend him, Tughra was a bitter man, the opium probably adding to his ill feelings. He used to satirize almost everyone: Kashmiri poets came in for his criticism and rebuke too. Irritated by his pretensions, Kashmir's most celebrated Persian poet, Mulla Tahir Ghani (Ghani Kashmiri), wrote a bitter reply:

> Tughra, whose soul is as base as his body,
> The jealous enemy of all pure-hearted men,
> Complains that poets steal his poems.
> They hate to utter his name, let alone poems.[3]

The first Mughal member of the court to be buried in the *mazar* was Hakim Amir Fathullah Shirazi (d. 1584), who in Mughal sources comes across as a close advisor and counsellor of Emperor Akbar. A polymath, the physician was also an accomplished astronomer and an inventor with a profound understanding of mechanics. He compiled treatises on multiple subjects, including logic, metaphysics, history, and a commentary on the Quran. Like most literati of his time, he composed some poetry, but he could best be described as a poet of mediocre quality. The hakim died from a high fever after he self-prescribed his cure, a rich, delectable dish of mutton-based porridge (*harissa*). Fathullah was initially buried in the compound of the Khanqah-i Maula, before a reburial at the *mazar*.

There is a view among Kashmiri historians that Mazar-i Shoura was established under Akbar. People in the city used to bury their dead at Malkah, the main Muslim cemetery of Srinagar. Alongside other older cemeteries in the city, Malkah stood in close proximity to areas of habitation. From the various *mohallas* of the city, a funeral procession could easily make its way on foot to Malkah. This practice was quite common for burials in the town till recent years. In the older *mohallas* of city, it is a pattern that is still followed. While Malkah served as a public cemetery, open to everyone in the city, prominent individuals tended to be buried in more historical cemeteries. These included the oldest Muslim graveyard in the city, Mazar-i Kalan, and the cemetery of the Shahmiri sultans, Mazar-i Salatin. Some would be buried in graveyards near the countless shrines and *khanqahs*; Khanqah-i Maula was a much sought-after and revered site.

Fathullah's reburial has been seen as evidence of the Mughal origins of the Mazar-i Shoura. During a documentation project on historical funerary landscapes in Kashmir, I had a chance to observe a few old tombstones that still survive in the *mazar*. Two of the oldest date from the sixteenth century, when the Chak sultans ruled Kashmir. One of the tombstones is inscribed with the names of twelve imams revered by Shia Muslims and a devotional prayer, also of Shia origin. This would indicate that the Mughals appropriated an older burial site in order to establish their cemetery of the poets.

While Srinagar was a city marked by the presence of leading Persian poets in the seventeenth century, today hardly anyone in the city is conversant with the language. Few remember the poets who had arrived in the city or are buried here. The *mazar*, once famed in literary circles from Srinagar to Tehran, stands forgotten. It lacks even simple signage to guide visitors.

# 12

# RAGHUNATH MANDIR

DECADES AFTER KASHMIRI PANDITS had left Srinagar, I visited a temple located in the heart of the city. Raghunath Mandir is unlike any other historical Kashmiri temple. The architecture borrows, imitates and replicates temple prototypes found in the northern plains of South Asia. With the curvilinear form of its *shikhara* (spire), once covered with metal sheets salvaged from biscuit boxes, the temple has more in common with its namesake in the city of Jammu than any traditional Kashmiri temple. The temple was built in 1875 by Maharaja Ranbhir Singh (r. 1856–1885), the second Dogra king of Kashmir. In 1835, twelve years before he was to be made Maharaja of Jammu and Kashmir by the British colonial authority, Ranbhir's father, Raja Gulab Singh (r. 1846–1856), then serving as an important functionary at the Lahore *durbar* of Maharaja Ranjit Singh (r. 1801–1839), laid the foundation of a temple at Jammu, the ancestral fiefdom of the Dogra rajas. The temple was named Raghunath Mandir and was dedicated to Lord Ram, the warrior-king, who remains perhaps the most popular incarnation of Lord Vishnu. Like many other princely houses in colonial India, Gulab Singh claimed descent from the Ram, who was both the presiding deity and the progenitor of the royal family. With the inauguration of Gulab Singh as maharaja of the newly created princely state of Jammu and Kashmir, Srinagar saw the infusion of cultural elements and religious traditions linked to the Dogras' court, which in turn were borrowed from the Sikh court of Lahore, Punjab.

The first temple to be consecrated by the Dogras at Srinagar is Gadadhar Temple, again a temple dedicated to Vishnu, which was built in the heart of the Sherghari, once the citadel of Afghan rulers of Kashmir. Like the Karkotas', the Dogra house also tried to recast Kashmir as a "Vaishnavite land". The commissioning of temples dedicated to the deity was a conscious attempt in this direction, though in the end it failed to reshape the native Hindu community. However, the transfer of this new cultural and artistic tradition from the plains was not new. Even earlier, when Ranjit Singh's army had freshly arrived in Kashmir, marking an end to five centuries of uninterrupted Muslim rule, one of the initial acts of the new rulers was the construction of two temples in the city, the Anandeshwar Temple at Maisuma, right opposite the royal citadel of Sherghari, and the Devi Temple at Pokhribal on the site of the former Mughal city of Naagar Nagar. Both were constructed in the same year, 1820, by Kashmir's first Sikh *subedar*, Diwan Moti Ram. Both the temples were commissioned around a natural feature, a spring (*nag*, in Kashmiri), which was traditionally revered by the Hindu and Muslim citizenry of the city. Yet the architecture of the temples is of Punjabi origin. Interestingly, both sites still retain the original chronograms written in Persian. The one at Maisuma reads:

> With the grace of Shivji, Shri Ram, and the King whose name is Nanak
> His benevolent shadow falls over the head of Ranjit Singh
> It was one thousand eight hundred and seventy-seven when
> The foundation of this temple was laid by the powerful hand of Moti Ram
> 
> 1220 AH (1820 CE)[1]

While the Anandeshwar and Devi temples largely withstood the political turmoil in the region, the same is not true of Raghunath Mandir. Recently, the government renovated the temple, and the once-white walls were replaced by something more like canary yellow, though the engineers responsible would call it ochre.

## RAGHUNATH MANDIR

Similarly, the painted sheets that many in the past might have misconstrued as gilded gold have been repainted in a bright red: somewhere in between auburn and wine-red.

My first visit to the temple took place on a cold, grey winter evening. The temple compound, which once opened majestically to the Jhelum river, welcoming worshippers, was equally desolate, the site overgrown with stinging nettles, making the approach to the main building even more painful. The surrounding houses, once a part of a Pandit neighbourhood, were slowly disintegrating, one element at a time: a window missing here, a wall crumbling there, a door long burnt. Historical ruins are generally impressive, but it would have required some imagination to be impressed by the view: it was as depressing as it gets. The main temple chamber is surrounded by a corridor—the *parikrama*, used by devotees to circumambulate the inner sanctum. Hindus perform the *parikrama* in a clockwise direction, a practice that is repeated even at Muslim shrines of Kashmir, whose plans borrow from those of a temple, with the saint's burial place replacing the site of the idol chamber. Historically, Muslims circumambulate (*tawaf*) the Kaaba at Mecca in an anticlockwise direction. Does the Kashmiri Muslim performance replicate an age-old Hindu ritual? Some would argue that the practice was adopted, to differentiate a local, non-sacrosanct ritual from a prescribed rite of hajj pilgrimage. Muslim day-to-day culture in the city borrows from both the Buddhist and Hindu past, in a myriad of ways and manners which are representative of the syncretic roots of the city's culture and functioning.

When I visited, in one corner of the temple corridor, a group of young boys—probably teenagers—were squatting tightly together around a makeshift fire, playing cards and smoking what I assume was *charas* (cannabis). People in the city generally like to talk; we like to converse. So, after some time, the uncomfortable silence ceased. We spoke: they, the only housekeepers of an abandoned temple, and me, an unwanted intruder. I must have sounded overwhelmingly patronizing with my countless inane questions. Some they answered, and some they chose to ignore, typical of the way teenagers navigate their conversations outside their peer groups: with a cycle of monosyllables, extended moments of silence, and then rapid bursts of meaningful sentences. The once-whitewashed walls of the corridor were black from soot and smoke, all indicators of the numerous fires around which the boys must have sat and smoked. Not so the main sanctum, the *garbhagriha*, where once the missing idols used to be. The floor of the sanctum bore no trace of fire. I asked the boys if they ever took refuge in the sanctum and if they ever smoked there, and the answer was "no". Why? One of them replied: "*Aati eas yim paran.*" (They [Hindus] used to read [pray] here.)

# 13

# THE BUND

*Here the native town ceases, and only large business houses or the dwellings of Europeans are to be found on the right bank of the river; rows of poplar shade the path, chinar-trees and gay flowers grow in the garden.*

Margaret Cotter Morison,
*A Lonely Summer in Kashmir* (1901)

A MAJORITY OF SRINAGAR'S inhabitants, albeit mostly Muslims, hold a dim view of the century-long Dogra rule. Nevertheless, the mid-part of the Dogra rule, starting with the long reign of Maharaja Pratap Singh (r. 1885–1925), marks the making of modern Srinagar. To a large extent, many of the projects that characterize this transformation were directed and overseen by the British Resident, who had a major hand in the running of the *durbar*. A Council of Regency had taken over the administration of the princely state after the maharaja was divested of most of his powers in 1889 on charges of collusion with Tsarist Russia. This accusation was a fabrication, but in the longer run the rule of this council proved far more beneficial to the modernization of the state than the timid and religiously conservative maharaja could ever have provided. So it was, under the watchful eyes of the Residents, that various welfare schemes were set up. Some were purely political, required for ease of administration and ruling, but they did make a change to the life of the city people. Srinagar might not be civilized enough, but for many Europeans making their way into the city, it had the essentials of civilized living: tap water, electricity, the telegraph, banks, European merchandise, and, after the completion of the Jhelum Cart Road in 1889, a motorable road, as well as two churches. There was also a hospital in the city run by Christian missionaries and a government maternity hospital, inaugurated on the occasion of the Diamond Jubilee of Queen Victoria.

Sometime in the early 1930s, the Russian traveller and exile Pavel Stepanovich Nazaroff undertook an arduous journey to the city across Central Asia and the Karakoram mountain range. Nazaroff was escaping from Kashgar, and life in Srinagar, after years of exile in Central Asia, would, he hoped, bring him to the "threshold of European civilization". While, for many, expectations never meet reality, this was not the case for Nazaroff, who after arriving in Srinagar wrote that "There was electric light everywhere and no doubt it was quite cheap, as I saw lamps burning in the shops in broad daylight. I saw taps too. Taps ... that means water laid on! What a contrast with Tashkent and Samarkand [...] Long avenues of handsome trees, broad playing-fields covered with turf, flower beds, villas."[1]

In *Kashmir and Kashghar*, a travelogue written much earlier, around 1873/4, the writer, a colonial officer, HW Bellew, makes the reader aware of a changing Srinagar, linking improvements to the city architecture and the cityscape to the colonial project of "civilizing the native". "New houses rising on the river frontage—very welcome signs, in their elaborate finish and straight angles and neat lines, of the march of civilization and adoption of modern improvements."[2]

So it was that the city kept on expanding incrementally, in pockets of new buildings: some public, a few recreational or institutional, but mostly residential, built on any piece of available land. Most of this new development took place in the vicinity of the mile-long avenue connecting Amira Kadal to the Rustam Garhi hillock. This marked the new so-called civil lines of the city, where the governing elite would be housed. At one end of it stood the Kashmir Club, a privileged Europeans-only club, next to the Residency. Then came the sprawling European quarters, constructed on the site of the *jagir* of the last Sikh *subedar* in Kashmir, Shaykh Imam al-Din. Here were set up many independent bungalows for the comfort of visiting European officials. The less fortunate, mostly soldiers and bachelors, were asked to camp near the banks of the Tsunth Kul (Apple Canal), a little further down: this was how far the European notion of "purdah" would operate.

The Residency kept a strict eye on the Europeans visiting the city. Despite the fun and the gaiety, the pervading mood was of Victorian sobriety. Although the colonials were supposed to set a fine and "superior" example of civilized behaviour for the natives, there were still scandals that managed to break out. Initially, the colonial visitors, escaping from the scorching heat of the land that was the British Raj, were provided with free accommodation in the bungalows. Today, the colonial name lies forgotten: the neighbourhood goes by the name of Shaykh Bagh, and the bungalows are all also long gone. The only reminder of that era is the Residency, functioning as an emporium, selling curios to interested visitors.

In 1903, the city was devastated by a flood, the first causality of which was the European quarter located upstream. It also took a heavy toll on the old city. To protect the city against any future catastrophe, a scheme was launched for strengthening the riverbanks by constructing masonry retaining walls. This also resulted in the creation of the first promenade in the city along the Jhelum, from Amira Kadal all the way up to the Club building. This promenade, The Bund, was an exclusive European area, with shops and banks catering to their needs.

The arrival of European visitors in the city during the last quarter of the nineteenth century resulted in the introduction of the Kashmir art phenomenon. Visitors would be taken by the city merchants to their residences, where they displayed their wares. Initially, what was on display was the famed Kashmiri shawl, but soon other decorative and utilitarian objects of silver, walnut wood and papier mâché were added to the list. The residence of the merchant trader served as the showroom, where over tea he would display his merchandise. The showroom business was mostly located in and around the Fateh Kadal bridge, even though Maharaja Ranbhir Singh had constructed a new centralized market near Saraf Kadal, in the heart of the city, but most showroom owners refused to move there. After a fire at Fateh Kadal destroyed many of the residences, some of the leading showrooms relocated to the Bund. The Bund showrooms came to display the best craft of Kashmiri artisans, and the showroom owners were valued for the excellence of their goods. A few old showrooms still survive on the Bund, practising a business that once made the city, and Kashmir, famous in many parts of the world.

Meanwhile, the city continued to expand in the vacant lands surrounding the European quarters, mostly on the left bank. A new palace, Gulab Bhawan, was constructed in the foothills of the Zabarawan mountain, overlooking the Dal Lake. The royal family vacated the Sherghari, and with that the last vestiges of physical contact between the old city and its rulers ceased to exist. This is the reality of the city even today. Moreover, once the rulers had moved, the people also began migrating from the older, densely populated parts of the city. The first to do so were those close to the court, many resettling in newer colonies emerging in the suburbs. The city's morphology was changing: the ruling elite would live in areas far removed, physically and visually, from the common masses, in areas with wider and better roads, and better access to services provided by the state.

In 1886 Srinagar received the grant of a municipality, and in 1934 Kashmir got its first elected assembly of the people.

# THE BUND

Both would function with limited power: in the case of the municipality, from the very outset its work would be questioned, and its functionaries accused of corruption and, occasionally, communalism. Despite this, as most observers of the city have commented, life improved. Streets were paved and provided with lighting. Cleanliness and hygiene, a concern of both the colonial authorities and the Christian missionaries, became ingrained in the functioning of the municipality. The dread of cholera and plague, which had resulted in numerous deaths in the past, was gone. A sewer line, the Green Line, named after its engineer, was laid in parts of the city where the ruling elite were housed—the civil lines. A new market modelled on the European high street was set up at Amira Kadal, and named after the maharaja, Hari Singh High Street. The municipality also undertook the construction of new metalled roads and parks in the city, two of which, at Shaykh Bagh and Nursingarh, were reserved for women. And, five years before India's independence in 1947, the first planned housing colony in the city was established, named Karan Nagar, after the heir apparent Karan Singh. Like much of the new development in the city, it was based on European planning principles, consisting of radial housing with straight lanes, green parks and a clear, clean geometry. This would be a plan repeated in many other planned colonies of the city. But that is a tale for another book.

# 14

# CITY ON A MAP

SOMEWHERE IN THE EARLY 2000s, a Japanese couple who were trekkers arrived at the office of the director general of tourism. The visit marked the slow revival of tourism in Kashmir, which had once been seen as a major industry during a period of steady increase from the 1960s through the 1980s. The office was located in the heart of the city's civil lines, in a spacious building with a large open quadrangle in the middle, popularly known as the TRC (Tourist Reception Centre). While government buildings in Srinagar tend to be shabby, dark and gloomy spaces, the TRC was airy and spacious: a modern brick-and-wood construction without any ornamental frills, but respectable and decently elegant. The building also displayed many old images of the city and Kashmir and contained a unique wall-length mural, the work of a Kashmir master, Ghulam Rasul Santosh. Before it was burned in a militant attack in 2005, many visitors to the city would arrive at the TRC to seek information on places to visit, collect brochures, and obtain permits for trekking. The building also housed the sole airline's office in the city and banking facilities.

On the walls of his chamber, the director general had a trekking map of Kashmir. The Japanese couple asked for a copy, but it was unavailable. They asked if they could take a photo of the map, but this was politely declined. The border of the framed map was marked with a small seal in the corner, saying that use of the map was "restricted". So, the couple left, and after a fortnight or so, on their return, they arrived at the TRC again, to pay a courtesy call. The trek had gone well, and people had been extremely helpful to them. When leaving, they gifted the director general with a map, an almost similar-looking map of Kashmir to the one on his wall, prepared by the US Central Intelligence Agency.[1]

Map-making has always been a dubious political exercise. A vast majority of people in India are unaware of the true shape of the country. The northernmost tip, the one which represents Ladakh and Kashmir, looks nothing like what is depicted on maps, especially those reproduced in school textbooks. After all, it is in schools that we acquire our formative understanding of our nation and what its physical appearance.

Modern cartography in South Asia traces its roots to the British, for whom it was a colonial exercise to gain more knowledge about the natives. Many of the native states were wary of the surveys the British conducted and rightly perceived that they would be instrumental in expanding British power and authority. The exercise was fuelled as much by the desire to map knowledge as to expand the empire. After their victory at the Battle of Plassey (1757), the British established a firm hold in India, and the exercise in empire-building began in earnest. This was accompanied by the surveying and mapping of the newly acquired territories in much of Bengal and Bihar. In 1802 the Great Trigonometrical Survey started in earnest and in 1875 it became the Survey of India. The map we used to work with as students in schools and colleges was usually a survey map from 1970 or 1975. These maps also formed the base maps on which planners and architects mapped the future expansion of cities all over India.

In *Survey of Kashmir and Jammu, 1855 to 1865*, Colonel RH Phillimore explained in detail how the Great Trigonometrical Survey started its work in Kashmir in 1855, with the full support of the native court. This support continued even during the Great Revolt of 1857 when the fate of British power in India was uncertain. By 1863 a survey of Srinagar and the surrounding areas, overseen by Lieutenant Montgomerie, had been completed and published. Montgomerie's city map was expanded by the London publisher John Murray in 1929, and included a depiction of the main street networks and major residential neighbourhoods. The new Murray map was made for the benefit of European readers, to act as a guide, so it is labelled with the names of places that would be of interest to visitors. These include the Residency, English Church, Post Office, Imperial Bank of India, Mission Hospital, Nedou's Hotel, Christian Missionary School, and shops on the Bund that catered to Europeans in the city: Dhanji Bhai, Lambert and Cockburn's. Aside from the Mughal gardens and a few monuments in the city, other significant places that gained recognition on the map included the silk factory, a distillery, the Zenana Hospital (a women's hospital) and a leper asylum. All of these sites were colonial interventions in the city's geography—a sign of modernity. The earlier Montgomerie map, on the other hand, is more detailed in its named descriptions of both natural landmasses and toponyms of neighbourhoods and religious sites.

There are some maps that predate the arrival of the Great Trigonometrical Survey. These early works were amateur exercises; often verbose, they inclined towards a more aesthetic representation with a tendency to sensationalize. This is true of the map drawn by François Bernier. As the first European representation of Kashmir, Bernier's map gives the impression of a drawing done for *The Lord of the Rings*, with Srinagar occupying the middle of a vast empty field ringed by a jagged mountain range. A pair of hillocks stand like brooding sentinels at either end of the city limits, one of which is identified as the Takht-i Sulaiman and the other as Hari Parbat. As Susan Gole observes in her study of Indian maps, the drawing is "far from accurate".[2] In fact, it is dismally wrong.

Srinagar was also represented in native maps, one of which is the so-called Jaipur Map, which has been tentatively dated by

Gole to the eighteenth century. This was a time when Mughal rule in Kashmir was on its last legs, and imperial investment in the city was gradually declining. Unfortunately, the Jaipur Map is locked in a custodial battle involving the trustees of the Jaipur City Palace, and the image we have in Gole's book is too grainy to reveal any interesting detail. Overall, the map confirms what historical texts from the period have recorded. It provides a fairly accurate idea of the city. The Jhelum is crossed by five bridges,[3] at least one of which houses shops. Major urban landmarks include the Nallah Mar canal running parallel to the Jhelum, the vast open ground of Idgah on the city's western edge, and the Mughal additions: Naagar Nagar and the gardens forming the northern periphery. These are all depicted with great precision in terms of how they locate the city's geography. Monuments that figure prominently on the map include the Jamia Masjid, Aali Masjid, Pather Masjid, Khanqah-i Maula, the Hazratbal shrine and the Thag Baba shrine. There is also a representation of a structure which seems to be a temple but could easily be the Dumath, the domed mausoleum within the Mazar-i Salatin. Although the map is not based on a scaled projection, it does convey the idea of a densely built area in the vicinity of the Jhelum and the Nallah Mar canal, which then gradually opens up as we approach Naagar Nagar.

The Jaipur Map is painted on cloth. In the nineteenth century, the same idea was also conveyed in a different and far more luxurious medium: the quintessential pashmina shawl of Kashmir. We have no idea where the idea originated of producing a shawl map of Srinagar, but the result is unique. At least four were commissioned. Today, these shawls are to be found in three different public museums: the National Gallery of Australia, in Canberra; the Victoria and Albert Museum, London; and the SPS Museum, Srinagar. One of the shawls was gifted to Queen Victoria by the Maharaja of Kashmir, Ranbhir Singh, and has a legend, "Skeleton Map of Kashmir", embroidered on the border. In addition to highly detailed information about the city, the map includes small inset maps of major tourist attractions in Kashmir, like the Achabal Bagh, the Verinag Bagh, and the Martand Temple. Unlike the other map shawls, this one is labelled in English, which supports the idea that it was presented to the Queen. This series of shawl maps, produced by the natives themselves, seeks to represent the city on a model quite different from European notions of cartography with their focus on scale and accurate projections. For the Kashmiri maker of the shawl map, the aim was not to show *how* the city is, but rather *what* the city is.

# II

# CITY AND LIFE

# 15

# AN ASSEMBLY OF POETS

MUGHAL RULE IN KASHMIR represented a unique cultural time in the city, opening up new vistas of cultural exploration and synthesis, as well as marking an advancement in urbanity. On the surface, Srinagar under the Mughals emerged as a vibrant cosmopolis. The Mughals had both the resources and the desire to recreate Kashmir in an image that conformed to their notions and principles of aesthetics: the Mughal *tarah*. Ideas, designs, motifs and practices originating at the royal cities of Agra, Delhi and Lahore were transmitted and replicated within an extremely short period at Srinagar, marking a successful movement of cultural capacities from the centre to a distant periphery like Kashmir. Aside from Mughal royalty and nobles, poets, diplomats and merchants at the Mughal court made their way to the city. These included individuals not only from Persia but also Turks, Armenians, Georgians and the very first Europeans to arrive in the city. While for some it was curiosity that drew them, to see for themselves the famed "paradise of the Mughal Empire", others used the occasion to trade. Some arrived as administrators, some to escape the heat of the Indian plains, and some were officially commissioned by the court to pen odes in praise of the empire and its paradise.

In the collection of the Royal Asiatic Society of Great Britain and Ireland, an illuminated manuscript completed on 26 Dhu 'l-Hijja 1073 AH (1 August 1663 CE) captures the allure that Kashmir held for literati at the Mughal court. Commissioned by Nawab Zafar Khan Ahsan (d. 1672), the manuscript includes two of his *masnavis* in Persian, "*Maikhanah-i Raz*" and "*Jilwah-i Naz*". Aside from being an accomplished poet, Zafar Khan was a prominent noble in the Mughal court. Both Zafar and his father, Khwaja Abul Hasan Turbati, served as *subedar* of Kashmir. The younger Khan was also an accomplished arborist who introduced various flower and fruit species in the gardens of Kashmir. The royal garden of Shalimar at Srinagar, which had been established by Emperor Shah Jahan as a young prince, was extended by Zafar Khan. During his first tenure as the *subedar* of Kashmir, Zafar constructed four gardens within a brief span of four months, though no trace of them survives today. To a large extent, Zafar mirrors the achievements and accomplishments of another Mughal noble, Abdul Rahim Khan-i Khanan (d. 1627).

It was at the invitation of Zafar Khan that Saib Tabrizi (d. 1676), the celebrated Persian poet whose work commanded great admiration in the court of the Safavid shahs of Iran, arrived in Kashmir. The two had earlier met in Kabul, where Zafar had been previously assigned as the *subedar*. While the Mughal *subedar* served as a generous patron of his senior contemporary, Saib in turn proved to be a confidant who guided Zafar in the subtleties of the craft of poetry making. A prolific composer—some accounts speak about a *diwan* (poetical composition) of 200,000 verses—Saib was regarded as a master in the choice of words, and his ideas and imagery helped create verses that still find admirers in the Persian-speaking world. Zafar Khan's company also provided Saib with an opportunity to visit Kashmir, a land that was already celebrated in Persian poetry at the Mughal court. Years after leaving Mughal India, Saib would continue his links with Zafar, exchanging letters with his one-time protégé, reminiscing about the times spent together. In Kashmir, the splendour of the city and the pomp of Zafar Khan's court moved the Iranian to write:

> *Saib*, I would lift my head in the breeze of paradise,
> Should fate destine me to reside in the City of Kashmir

## AN ASSEMBLY OF POETS

To return to the richly illuminated manuscript, it includes seven paintings, one of which depicts a *majlis* (assembly or gathering) hosted by the *subedar* in his *haveli* at Srinagar. The painter has successfully captured the physiognomy of the participants, highlighting the diverse mix of ethnicities and faiths in the *majlis*. A young Zafar Khan, seated on a carpet and smoking from a hookah, is in deep discussion with a group of poets, two of whom at least seem to be native Kashmiris. Books are lying open, adding to our impression of a deep and intimate literary discussion. A copyist is listening attentively to the conversation, while a troupe of musicians play on the edges of the assembly, setting the mood for the scene. The unnamed elderly painter of this illustration, wearing an eyepiece, has also placed himself in the scene along with the tools of his craft—a leather satchel, paints and brushes. A window in the chamber provides a brief glimpse into the world outside, contrasting the rich, ornate interior of the Mughal *haveli* with the Kashmiri landscape outside, which seems to quietly merge with the mountains and vegetation of the background. A series of houses, each within walled compounds, completes the Kashmiri scene. High compound walls, in brick or stone masonry, or even a simple wooden screen, were ubiquitous in the city landscape, and they still are, though in new materials and designs. Common to the city houses was a wall of rammed earth, famously known as *chini dous* (Chinese wall).[1] Does the name perhaps indicate the origin of this technique and element?

The compound wall is a city element, though in the rural landscape they were less common, for houses here shared compounds, and the fields were marked by borders, not by walls. In the home I grew up in as a child, a house built by my grandfather in the heart of the old city, there was an external compound wall, and then there were walls marking the front garden, the kitchen yard, and the backyard housing the store for cattle and firewood. This was largely the case too at my maternal grandfather's house, which had been built much earlier, in 1847. As a child, it was rather fascinating moving from one walled piece of land to another. This practice has declined, at least in the new suburbs of the city, but the high compound wall survives—sentinel of a tradition most people link with a desire for privacy (*purdah*). In the 1990s, when armed conflict erupted in the region, many residents in the city increased the height of these walls, seeking protection from the trouble on the streets outside. Whether for privacy or protection, the walls depicted in the Mughal painting have survived. Overall, however, the visuals of Srinagar are reduced in this painting to a mere caricature, subsumed within the larger verdant landscape.

The illustration, much like the general Mughal outlook, is simultaneously both celebratory and dismissive of Kashmir and the city. This is equally true of the *subedar* Zafar. On Shah Jahan's birthday, when most court officials would have been busy presenting the emperor with costly and unique gifts, Zafar petitioned for the removal of the oppressive practices and taxes imposed on the people of Kashmir. The royal proclamation that authorized this remission still occupies a prominent place on the main southern door of the Jamia Masjid at Srinagar. Yet, in one of his verses, the poet-administrator complains about the company of inarticulate Kashmiris.

We have no way of knowing who all were present in the *majlis*. Some historians are of the view that the practice of holding these literary assemblies in Srinagar was introduced by Zafar Khan, imitating a similar custom in vogue at the royal capital of Shahjahanabad (Delhi). Once established, the practice would continue under the Mughals and, following them, the Afghans and the Sikhs. Before long, dancing girls started to accompany the musicians, reciting verses from the *diwan* of the celebrated Persian poet Hafiz Shirazi. This choice of poet also gave the dancers their popular name—*hafizas*—and the *majlis* was referred

# AN ASSEMBLY OF POETS

to as Hafiz Nagma. When, in the nineteenth century, Kashmir saw a steady influx of colonial officials, the local court began to entertain the visitors, and the *hafizas* would be asked to perform. Oblivious to the origin of this performance, the Europeans started to refer to the *hafizas* as "nautch girls", a slur that implied the women were courtesans.[2] Most of the performances used to take place in the pavilion that Shah Jahan had constructed at Shalimar Bagh. This was also renamed the "nautch house".

In the summer of 1864, the British photographer Samuel Bourne arrived in Srinagar. His images capture, in great detail, the natural landscape and a few of the city's main monuments. A special focus of the photographer was the Shalimar Bagh; his images of the garden are of great archival value in understanding the change that has taken place both in the architecture and the landscape. Luckily enough, Bourne also captured some images of the "nautch girls" performing or posturing in the *bagh*. The pictures depict graceful women, resplendent in their finery. Ishaq Khan in his *History of Srinagar City* reproduces a textual description of their garments: "A tight-fitting short blouse and a skirt of enormous width which was worn gathered tightly about the waist. A dupatta of flimsy gauze-like silk was draped about her head and shoulders. She wore the traditional Kashmiri jewellery, large *kundlas* or earrings, talraz, Balis and necklaces."[3]

Gradually succumbing to shifting social and cultural practices and the changing nature of patronage, the once literary space of Hafiz Nagma became synonymous with an assembly of courtesans. The *hafizas* were performers or artisans, but soon their image became that of a prostitute. And, as a reformers in the city started a campaign against prostitution, people in the city stopped inviting the *hafizas* to perform.

In Srinagar, the arrival of the Mughals coincided with the establishment of the Urdu Bazaar, a neighbourhood and marketplace favoured by the Mughal soldiers. Across the

Mughal Empire, the Urdu Bazaar was synonymous with the flesh trade. This was also true of Srinagar. The area, also known as Tashwan, was the first red-light district in the city. There were other neighbourhoods equally infamous for prostitution, all in close proximity to the Sherghari. These included Suthra Shahi and Maisuma. In the first quarter of the twentieth century, as a response to Christian missionary work, Kashmiri Muslims also adopted a programme of reform. This affected the cultural matrix of the city, and as the city changed, the performances of the *hafizas*, sadly, also came to an end.

# 16

# SAINT OF THE CITY

*Shaykh Hamza Makhdum, "Oh! Mir Haidar, when there was nothing, what was?"*
*I replied, "That which was."*
*The Shaykh then asked, "When I will be there, what will be?" and I said, "That which will be, but I won't be."*
*The Shaykh then asked, "When He will be, where will you go?" I replied, " I will leave."*
*Then Shaykh asked, "Where will we search for you?" and I said, "From Him, only."*
*To which the Shaykh asked, "Who will find you, from Him?" I said, "A Ghaus (Helper)."*
*Then my Shaykh asked, "Oh! My Haider, did you find God?" and I said, "Oh! Murshid-i Azam (Great Teacher), I saw God but could not see my Self, and whenever I saw, it was not with these eyes."*

Baba Haidar Tulmuli, *Hidayat-al Mukhlisin*

IF SOMEONE COULD EVER claim to be the patron saint of Srinagar, based on popularity in the city, then it would certainly be the Suhrawardiyya Sufi Shaykh Hamza Makhdum. The shaykh was not an inhabitant of the city; he hailed from a village, Tujjar, in North Kashmir. Early in his childhood, he made his way to the city, enrolling in one of the religious establishments there. Life as a novice in a *khanqah* or *madrassa* revolved around work, worship and study. The food was simple and frugal, provided by an endowment or sourced through the charity of the court or the city merchants. There were few, if any, moments of leisure. But the young Hamza seems to have enjoyed this way of living, and as he grew up, he was drawn more and more into a life of asceticism. He remained celibate throughout his life, avoided the court and court life, and remained devoted to a life of severe penance and frugal eating habits.

While all these qualities qualified him for a saintly position, this was not the sole reason for his popularity. At the time when Hamza's fame was spreading, political authority in Kashmir was being transferred from the Shahmiri dynasty to the Chaks. Unlike the Shahmiris and a vast majority of Muslim Kashmiris, the Chaks adhered to the Shia branch of Islam. The patronage that Sunni men of religion had enjoyed now devolved on the Shia. Every act of omission was seen and judged through a sectarian lens. Soon, the Shia court was confronted by an opposing centre of authority, the Sunni religious classes. Shaykh Hamza emerged as the face of this Sunni opposition to Shia rule. This also became his main attraction, as the face of Sunni resentment.

In the city, Hamza was responsible for inaugurating the Suhrawardiyyas as a major Sufi order. Before his arrival, the city *khanqahs* were dominated by the Kubrawiyyas and, to a certain extent, the Nurbakshiyyas. Away from the city, the Reshi, a native order of Sufis, prevailed over much of the rural landscape. Unlike the Sufis in the city, who sought court patronage and adhered to the Persian language, the Reshi teachings were rooted in the vernacular. On his death, Hamza was buried in the foothills of Koh-i Maran, near the mall mosque where he had spent much of his life in prayer and devotion. A shrine was constructed over his grave by Emperor Akbar, though no Mughal source mentions this. Gradually, the small shrine evolved into a complex of multiple buildings, patronized by Mughal royalty, Afghan *subedars*, Kashmiri merchants, and the people of the city at large. To some, the architecture of this vast and layered complex may seem a bit eclectic, but there is a certain harmony to this vast enterprise, which occupies the entire southern foothill of Koh-i Maran.

## SAINT OF THE CITY

Endowment deeds, gifting land to the shrine, that bear the marks of Emperor Shah Jahan and Princess Jahanara Begum, are testimony to the appeal of the shrine and the saint among the Mughal royalty. From its height, the shrine complex, the largest in the city, dominates the cityscape while also offering its protection to countless devotees below.

# 17

# THE BAGH (GARDEN)

*My dear, [remember] the Iris in its full bloom,
when it's wailing in the air—when it dies down.*

Mirza Aboul Qasim (d. 1850s), "Marg" (Death)

*The flowers of Kashmir are beyond counting and calculation. Which ones shall I write of? And how many can I describe?*

Jahangir, *Jahangirnama*

IN THE CITY, TWO flowers can be seen growing wild on bits and pieces of open land still left unclaimed: narcissus (*nargis, yembarzal*) and iris (*sosan, mazar-i moundh*). For me, the narcissus is one of the most evocative harbingers of spring: an amazing, transient flower that marks the beginning of the new year. After the long and, at times, cold and grey winter, the scent of mounds of narcissi planted densely along slopes seems divine. The petite flowers are just big enough to make the eye linger as they sway delicately in the spring air. Traditionally, the narcissus is a flower of spring. From mid-February to late March, the various species of narcissus hold sway, though today, given climate change, you may find some bulbs blooming in early winter. Though it is possible that both the iris and narcissus were native to Kashmir, it was the Mughals who cultivated them within their *baghs*.

Yet for many in the city, narcissus, along with the iris, is generally avoided, for both are seen as flowers of the graveyard. There is a lingering hesitation in planting them in gardens. People refer to both as the *mazar posh* (flower of the cemetery).

This is equally true of the weeping willow, which goes by its Persian name of *bayid-i Majnun*, the tree of Majnun. The story of Majnun (crazy, in Arabic) is of Arab origin, and concerns a Bedouin poet, Qays, and his lover, Laila. The Persian poet Nizami Ganjavi (d. 1209) successfully transformed this desert tale of longing, loss and tragic death into a powerful symbol of unfulfilled love.

In Persian literature, *bayid-i Majnun* has been used as a symbol of human frailty. Someone must have been impressed by the long drooping branches of the willow tree to name it after the poet, who, in most paintings, is represented as an emaciated figure wandering in the desert, scantily clothed (or even naked) with long, dishevelled hair. In the cultural milieu that governed Srinagar, long hair in men was seen as a symbol of mental affliction, at times even of effeminate behaviour. So few dared to plant the tree in their homes.

It is to the Mughals that the city owes its love of gardens and planting. This is not to say that Srinagar was devoid of gardens before the coming of the Mughals. We have textual references that speak about gardens established by native rulers predating the Mughal *baghs*. Yet these descriptions fail to give us any idea of garden landscape, and their references to garden horticulture are insignificant and virtually nonexistent.

The aesthetics of the garden, which the city cultivated till recently, consciously chose to mimic the Mughal *baghs* or at least a semblance of those *baghs* that could be recreated with considerable economy and minimal labour. For many in the city, the idea of a garden was, and remains, a combination of beauty and considerable usefulness. Mulberry, quince, pomegranate and walnut are trees common to city gardens. Traditionally, pear and almond were more common in orchards on the city's periphery. After the demise of Mughal rule in Kashmir, as the former royal city of Naagar Nagar fell into disuse, large parts of

# THE BAGH (GARDEN)

it were converted into almond orchards. This was a long-drawn-out process. Simultaneously, the former royal gardens lining the adjoining Nigeen Lake, on the opposite side of Naagar Nagar, also assumed the form of almond fields.

In the numerous travelogues written by European visitors to the city in the nineteenth century, they speak about how orchards in the city outskirts are neither walled nor was their fruit sold; anyone who so desired could pick and eat. This may suggest abundance and plentifulness, a sure sign of prosperity, but that was not the case. After the Mughals, people in Kashmir were burdened with excessive taxation under the successive regimes of the Afghan, Sikh and Dogra rulers, whose governance was driven by the desire to exact maximum revenue.[1] Everything was taxed—land most of all. In such desperate circumstances, the upkeep of orchards was a sore challenge, and many owners allowed the land to fall into disuse. As a result, numerous orchards, once planted with great care, were gradually transformed into sites of idyllic wilderness, devoid of a caretaker or protector.

Within the city, a few gardens boasted a special grape, *dachh-i hussani*. This variety was considered a precious commodity and gardeners were unwilling to share it. Some believe that it was introduced by the Mughal *subedar* Zafar Khan, who, aside from being a good administrator and poet, was a keen horticulturist. Given the grape's origin in Afghanistan, where it is widely cultivated in regions of Herat, Kabul and Balkh, there is a lingering possibility that one of the Afghan *subedars* might have brought it to the city. Unlike the Mughals, the Afghan rulers of Kashmir were devoid of any grace; they were mostly seen as tyrants, a great affliction which the people had to endure. Yet there are a few exceptions, notably Amir Khan Jawan Sher. The young Amir Khan was a Qizilbash, member of a tribe that had once served as the personal force of the shahs of Iran.[2] He was also a major builder whose architectural enterprises rival that of

## CITY OF KASHMIR

Kashmir's most celebrated Mughal *subedar*, Nawab Ali Mardan Khan (d. 1657). Unlike the famously rich Mughal *subedar*, who was rumoured to possess the *sang-i faras* (alchemist's stone), Amir Khan had to make do with limited resources. So Kashmiri historians argue the Afghan *subedar* vandalized older Mughal *baghs*, many of which had already fallen into disuse, to construct his pleasure gardens.

The Afghan also transferred the seat of the provincial administration from Naagar Nagar to an area located a mile south of the existing city limits. The new citadel was named after its builder, Sherghari (The Citadel of the Lion), and marks the first major urban expansion on the left bank of the Jhelum. He also laid a bridge still bearing his name, Amira Kadal, to connect Sherghari with Takht-i Sulaiman along a wide, poplar-lined avenue. In the maze of twisting, turning alleys and streets of the city, this one-and-a-half-mile-long stretch was the first straight avenue—something the people of Srinagar would be eternally thankful for. The city was more used to a street network resembling "a complicated labyrinth of narrow and dirty lanes, scarcely broad enough for a single cart to pass".

City legends would have us believe that Amir Khan also intended to construct a wooden trellis (*jafri*) over the Jhelum near Sherghari. The intention was to design this watery course as a shady green arbour, with the vines of *dachh-i hussani* climbing over the trellis. A failed revolt against the Taimur Shah, the ruler of Afghanistan, ended both the pleasure-loving *subedar*'s stay in the city and his dreams and design experiments.

Meanwhile, in the city of my childhood, a grape vine was often left wild to grow over the compound wall, making its way into the neighbour's garden. An unwritten rule governed the collection of the produce: the one in whose compound the branch fell could take the fruit. A gardener I knew used to say fruit is meant to be shared, not hoarded or sold.

## THE BAGH (GARDEN)

Nevertheless, the garden of yesteryear was not simply a landscape of productivity. For a more ornamental appearance, it would be planted with cypress (*sarvi*) and Persian lilac (*yusman*). Both were indispensable to the Mughal landscape and featured prominently in Persian poetry. Though Jahangir was full of praise for the tulip (*gul-i lala*) planted in the city, in gardens and on the rooftops of houses, the fashion for planting tulips had almost died. The flower was seen as too delicate and short-lived, and few gardeners or homeowners felt it worthwhile to invest energy or money in its cultivation. In the wild, though, come spring, a native variety of deep red tulip would emerge from the ground, often at sites that had once housed the gardens of the Mughal royalty and nobility. Something in the city's temperament inclined people to judge and weigh every act in terms of its longevity and profitability. The poverty that engulfed Kashmir in the nineteenth century probably rendered the city conservative and cautious in its dealings. The need to hoard may result from greed, but it also articulates the fear of an uncertain future. Talking to elders in the city, you get a feel of how tough life was and how recent the city's prosperity is. Growing up in the 1950s and 1960s, many recall living through cholera, famine, fire, earthquake, flood and misgovernance. Survival required a degree of tenacity, not flamboyance. In the city, self-indulgence (*ayashi*) was seen as a vice; it represented a lack of fortitude. Srinagar certainly had its period of affluence; the city possessed wealth but was not ostentatiously rich. In present-day Srinagar, this, like much else, has changed. After a tulip garden was inaugurated in 2017, this delicate flower, a favourite of the Mughals, re-emerged in the gardens of the city as one of the most sought-after flowers.

Also found growing virtually wild in the gardens of the city was the damask rose, which, for Kashmiris, is simply the *koshur gulab*, the rose of Kashmir. Widely cultivated in the city, it was grown for the sweet fragrance of the flower rather than its appearance. At the Mughal court, the *itir* (perfume) of rose was much celebrated after it was accidentally discovered by the mother of Empress Nur Jahan (d. 1645). In Kashmir, the Mughals, including the empress, undertook extensive cultivation of the *gulab*, and some reports indicate that the petals of these roses were also a source of revenue. Three decades after the Mughals had lost Kashmir, the *koshur gulab* and its *itir* continued to be celebrated: "the *rose* of *Kashmir*, which, for its brilliancy and delicate of odour, has long been proverbial in the *east*; and its *essential* oil or ottar is held in universal *estimation*. The *season*, when the *rose first* opens in *blossom*, is celebrated with much *festivity* by the *Kashmirians*, who *report* in crowds to the adjacent gardens, and enter into *scenes* of gaiety and *pleasure*, rarely known among other *Asiatic* nations."[3]

What pleases one often fails to impress the other. A French botanist, Victor Jacquemont, arrived in the city in 1831, and spent most of the summer in Kashmir. Residing at Shalimar, the imperial garden, where once Jahangir and Shah Jahan had held court, he had the opportunity to observe the roses bloom in the garden. The display left the Frenchman unimpressed: "This garden is filled with roses in bloom; but they are small, and have but little fragrance."[4]

For the natives, though, cultivating roses also served a practical purpose. The petals found their way into making *gul kand* (sweet rose), a preserve that could be used to sweeten the local tea, *khawa*, or even spread on bread like marmalade. As a child, I would often steal it, scoop after scoop; the same happened with *muraba-i bihi* (the marmalade of the quince). Another common use of the rose was in making *gulab arak*, distilled rose water. Within the old city, a family of distillers, the Kozighars, continue to make *gulab arak*, operating from their ancestral shop. Here, shelves of bottles in green, amber, frosted, etched or plain glass, covered in dust and cobwebs, provide a tantalizing glimpse

## THE BAGH (GARDEN)

into a bygone era. The elderly shop-owner proudly points to filigree decanters of a European make that the family acquired a generation back. A majority of the bottles are today empty; the *gulab arak* is now packed and sold in cheap plastic bottles. The buyers are mostly locals.

Across the sacred landscape of Kashmir, on major religious festivals, the *arak* of rose is sprinkled among worshippers in finely wrought rose sprinklers (*gulab pash*) crafted from silver, brass or copper. This custom was more prevalent among the Muslim community. The *gulab pash* was treated as an heirloom and passed down in the family, much like the prized pashmina shawl. And, for the vast majority of people in the city who never owned one, you could always borrow from someone in the *mohalla*. The *gulab arak* also had a ceremonial use, as wedding guests, particularly the groom's party (*barat*), would be welcomed with it, but that tradition has now almost died out. A shower of cheap confetti seems to be the popular fashion these days.

The Kozighar shop is located near a major intersection of the old city, leading to one of Srinagar's iconic monuments, the Khanqah-i Maula. Many visitors to the *khanqah* make their way to the shop, which has gained some fame in recent years as a result of social media. The shop was also featured in the travel magazine *Condé Nast Traveller*. This has resulted in a small revival, as recently another family member opened an *arak* shop in the same building. Earlier, the family also made various herbal essences: *arak* was used in the Graeco-Persian system of medicine, the *unani*. But that tradition has declined. Talking to the present owners, you get the feeling that the knowledge behind this practice has not survived. Unfortunately, this is true of many professions and crafts that once made Srinagar a much sought-after craft market. I did try to ask the owner if they used to make distilled liquor, but he was deeply offended by the question. Drinking alcohol is forbidden—*haram*. Alcoholic distillation is nothing new; historically, *arak* was served as a social drink across the many geographies of the Muslim world. Perhaps even in Srinagar, sometime long, long ago?

There is a prevailing sense that the Mughals introduced the damask rose, cypress and lilac to Kashmir. Yet a reading of Jahangir's memoirs indicates otherwise. These flowers and trees feature prominently in the Persianate culture towards which the city sought to orient itself long before the coming of the Mughals. Borrowing from the Persian traditions, Kashmiri poetry is replete with similes, metaphors and symbolism relating to these flowers and trees. The cypress represents the slender, elegant stature of the beloved; the rose is a manifestation of divine glory or the face of the beloved; while the tulip and poppy symbolize a bleeding heart—loss, death.

In *A Suitable Boy*, a novel set in hot, scorching mainland India, Vikram Seth nicely captures some of the smaller nuances of everyday life. For instance, he labels certain flowers "bureaucratic". If I ever had a chance to compile such a list, pansy (*panzein*), zenia and snapdragon would definitively be on it. These three, along with calendula (*hamesha bahar*) and marigold (*gul-i jafar*, also *batti posh*), are permanent residents in any Srinagar garden, new or old. Given the limited confines of the city, most *mohallas* were densely built. Along the riverfront and on the streets, houses rub shoulder with one another, endlessly. Nevertheless, within each *mohalla*, one would come across a few detached houses, built on plots sufficiently large to fashion a city garden. Visiting Srinagar in 1822, William Moorcroft left a description of the city and the city gardens, both of which failed to impress him: "The houses of the better class are commonly detached, and surrounded by a wall and gardens, the latter of which often communicate with a canal: the condition of the gardens is no better than that of the building, and the whole presents a striking picture of wretchedness and decay."[5] In reply,

## THE BAGH (GARDEN)

one can argue Moorcroft never got an invitation to a regular Kashmiri mansion, or maybe he was not discerning enough. His visit also coincided with one of the worst times in the history of the city. Urban decay generally accompanies political anarchy and upheaval.

In the city, the garden, though, was never a single landscaped space; rather, it was compartmentalized into a series of smaller walled sections: the front lawn (*bagh* or *angun*), the backyard (*pout angun*), and the kitchen garden (*varr*). Those who grew up in the city before the 1980s would remember garden gates and compound walls covered with wild roses twining with the ivy, honeysuckle (*heither*) and morning glory (*ashq-i pechan*) in a vibrant, colourful collage—not a Monet but playful enough. There was a certain temptation these green walls held, something that made you reach out and touch—often simply a desire to cut or pick and run away with a flower. The modern boundary walls of brick and cement, on the other hand, seem aloof, distant, and wary of everyone in the street—a forbidding sentinel daring anyone to approach.

Growing wild in the fields and meadows bordering the city, hyacinth (*sonbul*), poppy (*khaskhash*), red poppy (*gulal*), violet (*gul-i bunafshi*) and daisies once reigned supreme. Within these semi-urban landscapes on the city's edge, Ustad Mansur, the chief painter at the court of Jahangir, discovered and painted a red tulip in the European manner and style. Today, the painting remains a prized possession in the collection of the Maulana Azad Library at Aligarh.

The picturesque was not limited to the meadows and gardens alone. Stately, tall poplars and rows of willow (*virh*) were usually planted along watercourses and lake edges. A notable exception to this waterside plantation was, and remains, the Jhelum. In the heart of the city, houses were constructed right up to the edge of the river; there was no green respite for travellers passing by on its turbid water. The few green spots that existed in the city were invariably near major religious or public landmarks: the Khanqah-i Maula, Sherghari, Raghunath Mandir. Outside the city limit, groves of chinar and willow lined the Jhelum as the landscape merged with the verdant countryside.

In 1890, a British Residency was established in Srinagar, in a part of the city that came to be known as the European quarters. The building was designed in the style of an English country manor house within an expansive garden lined with poplar trees. One of the occupants of the Residency, Sir Francis Edward Younghusband, during his three years as the Resident (1906–1909), oversaw the development of the garden, which he describes as "one of the most charming houses in India—a regular English country-house [...] Here grow in perfection every English flower."[6]

For the most part, the English flowers that Younghusband listed are native to Kashmir, yet the arrangement was typical of an English garden layout. Additionally, several new varieties of flowers, shrubs and trees were introduced into the garden and, by default, to the city. These included magnolias, hybrid tea roses, Californian poppies, pansies and strawberries. Those trees and plants, which in the Kashmiri landscape were traditionally confined to forests, meadows and fields, also made their way into this English garden. These included borders of iris, daffodil, crocus and the imperial crown lily, and groves of conifers, pines, elms and yews. When in the first quarter of the twentieth century the Dogra rulers began work on the conservation of the surviving Mughal gardens in the city, they acquired the technical help of British engineers working with the Archaeological Survey of India. Many newly introduced plant and tree species that had made their way into the Residency were also planted in the Mughal gardens, adding a new layer to a historical landscape that keeps evolving.

# THE BAGH (GARDEN)

In the new part of the city, which replicated the colonial civil line, a series of detached bungalows, each with a garden mirroring the Residency, was erected. Some served as the extension of the European quarters and were reserved for the Europeans, while others housed the growing body of non-native Indians working in the government. These new constructions, most of which were produced in the first half of the twentieth century, were built to imitate colonial architecture and the colonial landscape. Gradually, the British garden also made its way into the native *bagh*, a bit modified and scaled-down: the turfed lawn became as important as the planted flowers, neatly trimmed boxes of evergreen shrubs replaced the mud walls, and wooden lattices were used to act as garden separators. Finally, as a gesture of deference to the new, dominant culture, some people in the city began planting iris and narcissus in their gardens. A taboo had been broken, though the truth is, this was simply designed to impress the natives.

# 18

## SAEER (OUTING)

12. Mosque of Madni, Nau Shahr, Srinagar, 2019.
Photo © Zubair Ahmed.

13. Jamia Masjid, Srinagar, 2024.
Photo © Tabish Gazi.

14. Dumath, Srinagar, 2024.
Photo © Tabish Gazi.

15. Mulla Shah Mosque, Naagar Nagar, Srinagar, 2023.
Photo © Tabish Gazi.

16. 19th-century Ragunath Temple, Fateh Kadal, 2023.
Photo © Shoaib Qasba.

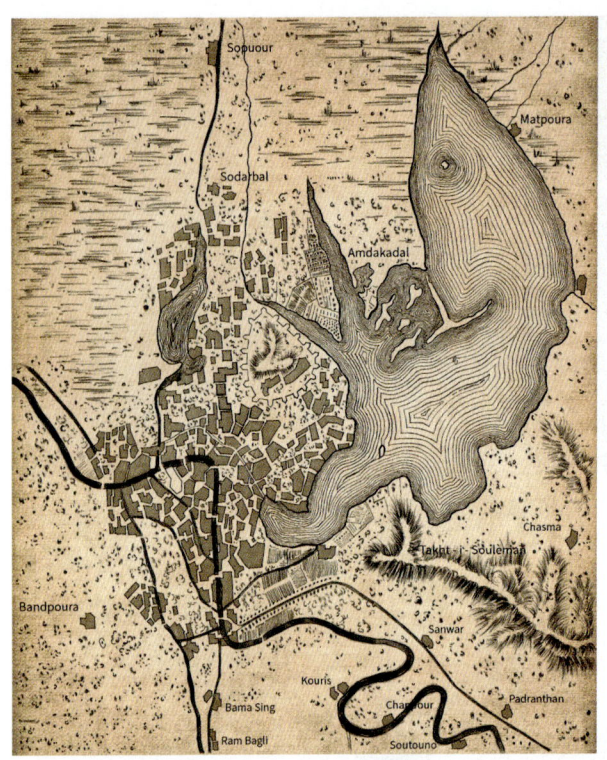

17. Colonial map of Srinagar based on C Perron (1885), pen and ink, 2023. Photo © Zoya Khan.

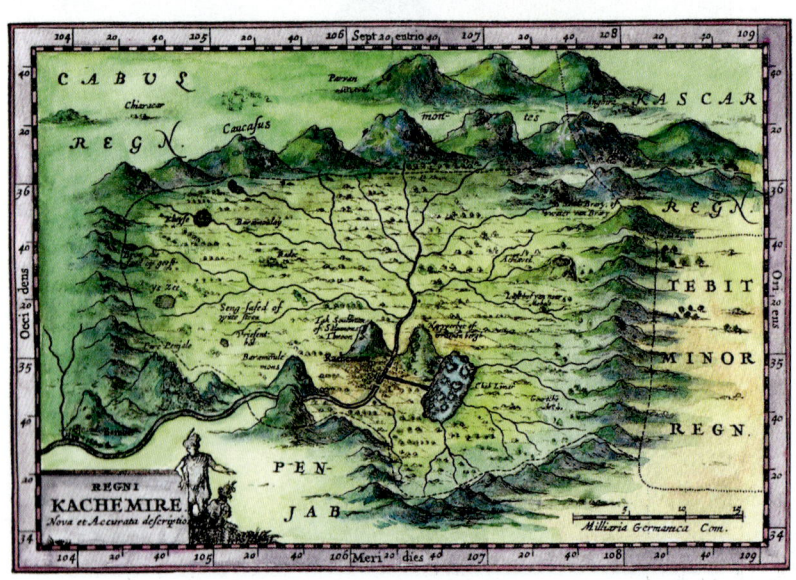

18. Kashmir, map based on François Bernier, watercolour, 2023. Photo © Basita Shah.

19. Sultan-al Arifin Shaykh Hamza Makhdoom, Kashmir School, 19th century, SPS Museum. Photo © Sameer Hamdani.

20. Streets and lanes of the downtown, Aali Kadal, Srinagar, 2025. Photo © Ta-Ha Mughal.

21. Kozghar shop, Khanqah-i Maula, Srinagar, 2024. Photo © Ta-Ha Mughal.

22. Pari Mehal, Mughal bagh built by Dara Shikoh, 17th century, Srinagar, 2014. Photo © Mukhtar Ahmad.

23. A city in flames, Nowhatta, Srinagar. Photo © Javed Dar.

24. '*How Shall I Remember My City?*', acrylic on canvas, 2024. Photo © Basita Shah.

*The Kashmirian are gay and lively people, with strong propensities to pleasure. None are more eager in the pursuit of wealth, have more inventive faculties in acquiring it, or who devise more modes of luxurious expense. When a Kashmirian, even of the lowest order, finds himself in the possession of ten shillings, he loses no time in assembling his party and launching into the lake, solaces himself till the last farthing is spent.*

George Forster, A Journey from<br>Bengal to England ..., vol. 2 (1798)

PEOPLE IN SRINAGAR LOVE to go out with family or with friends, and so the idle gossip passed to the English traveller George Forster (d. 1792) by a Georgian merchant is as true of the city today as it was in eighteenth-century Kashmir. To the English visitor, Kashmir came across as a land of escape and indulgence, where Muslims of Afghan, Turkish and Persian descent were no longer restrained by the sombre, dour mood of their Muslim faith prevalent in their home countries. Kashmir was a land of unbridled licence. Like most Europeans discovering the "Orient" in the eighteenth and nineteenth centuries, Forster's travelogue is filled with a great measure of racial prejudice and some conceit. It also displays a superficial understanding of native history and life. But Forster was not to blame: this was the mood of his time.

Most picnics in Srinagar tend to be joyous occasions set within a familiar rather than a formal setting. To a degree, this feature does provide valuable insight into Srinagar's urbanity. On the surface, this simple pleasure derived from a day spent away from the city seems to be an indictment of city life or, rather, the city itself. This desire to escape resembles perhaps a brief pause in the everyday grind and despair of city life.

In the local vernacular, we don't have a specific word that would describe the occasion, but *saeer* (from the Persian *sair*, to travel), *chakar* (in Hindustani, to move in a circle), excursion and picnic are commonly used. While the Persian, Punjabi and English terms indicate the foreign source of the borrowing, the desire is genuinely Kashmiri. In boats, *tongas* (carts), buses and then cars, people would travel to escape from the city. For a vast majority of the city's working class, who could ill afford the extra cost of hiring a boat or a *tonga*, walking was the only option. And so they made their way on foot to the nearest field for a day of ease, merriment and some indolence. For one day in the year, at least, life's constraints could be abandoned. There was no timekeeping for the day; it had a start and an end, and in between the day was what you wanted it to be: a time for conversation, food, tea or a smoke. You could remain under the same shade the whole day or else explore your surroundings. Nothing was determined.

Ordinarily, most Kashmiris live in the dread of winter: *wandi gos travun* (may the winter go easy on us) is a wish that captures this fear. In the past, winter was also a time of scarcity; nothing grew on the land, and people had to survive on whatever they could store: dried vegetables, some lentils, and mainly rice. Before 1896, the city had no tap water. Only the rich could afford to have water delivered to their doorsteps daily in leather bags and clay urns from springs located in the mountains across the city lake. A teacher in the city, Munshi Hasan Ali, has left an account of daily life in the city for the years between 1896 and 1907. In his memoir, he records how, in 1896, after a few failed attempts, tap water was finally supplied to the city on the occasion of Nauroz, the Persian New Year.[1] There were people in the city rich enough to develop a taste for water and judge its quality in a single sip. A connoisseur of water in the city acknowledged that the new tap water was "lighter than the water of the river Jhelum". The traditional way of judging water in Kashmir was by its *wazn*, or heaviness: the lighter the water, the better its taste and properties of digestion.

In the city, the occasion when tap water became available was a source of much joy and celebration, especially for women. In most households, it was women who would collect and bring the water. This could be the water of the Jhelum, one of the numerous water canals in the city or, for those lucky enough, a spring located in the neighbourhood. Like many burdens linked with home-making, this was a task that women would do alone, unaided. Even today, in some parts of rural Kashmir, it is a task that women perform every day.[2]

At home, barring the few rich, people had no means of heating their homes. The kitchen, with its open hearth, was the space where you cooked, ate and slept. Winter was also the season of diseases and, invariably, death. The pains of a Kashmiri winter can be traced in the poetry of Ghani Kashmiri, a recluse who was otherwise least inclined towards worldly comforts:

> Such is the nip in the biting air
> That the moist eye resembles a stony glass.
> Scared to their bones, now men are of water.
> Like the mirror, they hide it under the earth.
> ...
> The tear which drops from the crying eye
> Freezes like the wax dripping down the candle.
> ...
> This winter's tale I can no longer narrate
> For the tongue is now an icicle in my mouth.[3]

So, come spring, people from the city would slowly make their way to Koh-i Maran, the site of numerous Mughal *baghs* interspersed with the ruins of their palaces, mosques and *sarais* (rest houses). Early in the spring, the foothills would be covered with delicate almond, peach and apricot blossoms, forming a colourful spectacle. With the collapse of the Mughal authority, this sanctified area, once out of bounds for ordinary Kashmiris, became established as a popular picnic spot.

Also located on the summit of the hillock is a modest fort of no architectural pretensions. Constructed in 1811 by an Afghan *subedar*, Sadar Atta Muhammad Khan, the fort is testimony to the transient nature of Afghan architecture. An insipid structure that also proved politically inconsequential, the fort has no story that celebrates battle, blood or acts of valour. The Afghan *subedars* were always searching for a way out of their troubles, squabbling with the royal court in Kabul. When his former master, Shah Shuja (r. 1806–1809), lost the Afghan throne, Atta Muhammad invited him over to Kashmir and then imprisoned him in the fort in an act of betrayal. Perhaps the rebel *subedar* believed that the code of Afghan hospitality, *Pashtunwali*, did not extend to royal pretenders. This act of betrayal is the fort's only claim to glory.[4]

During my childhood, the fort would be opened to the public once a year to celebrate the Baisakhi festival, attracting a huge crowd, mostly of city dwellers.[5] Much earlier, in my father's youth, Bakshi Ghulam Muhammad used the same occasion and the same physical setting to organize a festival celebrating the almond blossoms in the city. As the serving prime minister (1953–1963) of Kashmir province, Bakshi had little popular support. He had won his position through a soft coup, deposing his mentor and the former prime minister, Shaykh Muhammad Abdullah (d. 1983). Seen as the agent of Delhi in Srinagar, Bakshi sought to quell popular discontent through a curious but effective mixture of fear, patronage and public celebrations.

## SAEER (OUTING)

Under Bakshi's ten-year rule, Kashmir was an experiment in how the state's largesse could manage public dissatisfaction and undermine political aspirations; this is how Hafsa Kanjwal views Bakshi's rule in her book *A Fate Written on Matchboxes*.

Many of those partying on the slopes of Koh-i Maran would end their day by stopping at the shrine of Shaykh Hamza Makhdum, to pay obeisance and offer prayers. For the Hindus, a visit to the Chakreshwari Temple, also located in the same area, completed the day's outing, though I believe this would have occurred only after Kashmir was transferred to the Lahore *durbar* of Maharaja Ranjit Singh. With this final act, the day would end as the party returned to the city through one of the numerous Mughal gates.

Those more adventurous would instead commit themselves to a day-long boat journey over the waters of the Dal Lake. A small boat or a plain barge (*donga*) would be hired to take the party to the many Mughal gardens on the other side of the lake. This included a visit to the Nishat Bagh, Shalimar Bagh, Naseem Bagh and the island garden of Char Chinari located in the middle of the lake. Those who could afford it would stay on the lake for days, sometimes for a week. Those whose *chakar* extended over a longer duration would complete the pleasure trip by paying respects at the Hazratbal shrine, Kashmir's most revered Muslim site. The shrine, once the site of a Mughal *bagh*, commands a fine view of the Dal Lake and the mountains framing its waters.

In the nineteenth century, we come across references to another tradition in the city, which highlights how easily the sacred and the profane could and did overlap. A riverine procession of boats and barges filled with families and friends would proceed from the city to the shrine of Sayyid Qamar al-Din Bukhari in the village of Ganderbal to participate in the annual *urs* (celebration of a saint). For many, the procession was part of the cycle that governed city life, a religious pilgrimage. But then there were also those, mostly youth, for whom the entire event was simply a *chakar*; their participation was not governed by a desire to engage in devotional practice. While engaging the services of singers to lighten the mood on the boats had a historical precedent, there were reports of people gambling their way into the night. Many saw the procession as an excuse to engage in wayward behaviour. A number of Muslim reformers were already challenging the shrine culture in the city; and so the procession was the perfect target for those who opposed it. The procession was presented as a disturbance of the city's piety; it was a means of circumventing the purity of religious practices and the morally upright behaviour that was desired by the reformers. Finally, as the region erupted into armed revolt in the 1990s, the procession was eventually cancelled.

Earlier in the city's modern history, as vehicular transportation replaced horse-driven carriages and river-based boats, people started moving further away from the traditional picnic spots. The British had popularized the hill station of Gulmarg, which, along with Pahalgam, became the new leisure spot to visit for the newly emerging middle class of the city. Even in its darkest hours, when life in the city came to a standstill and death reigned supreme, the tradition never died out. Some, like George Forster, would argue this speaks to the fickleness of the people. But the city would say: this is simply life.

# 19

# CHIRAGAN (ILLUMINATION)

IN HIS *WAQIAT-I KASHMIR*, the Kashmiri historian Khwaja Muhammad Azam Dedhmari writes about an extraordinary event that took place in the city during Ramzan, the Muslim month of fasting, in the year 1103 AH (1691 CE). It was summer, and an Iranian visitor in the city, Mir Husayn Sabzwari, had taken up residence on the eastern bank of the Dal Lake, at a site known as Gupkar. In seventeenth-century Srinagar, the entire lakefront extending from Gupkar to Shalimar comprised a series of gardens lining the lake's eastern shore, which belonged to the imperial family and leading nobles at the Mughal court. Owning a garden on the banks of the lake was a privilege, even though most gardens reverted to the emperor on the owner's death. In between the numerous *baghs* stood a few small villages, sparsely populated and settled by Kashmiris, the perfect representation of an arcadia. For the city dwellers, the lake provided a once-in-the-year opportunity for an excursion, a life beyond the grind of day-to-day existence. Though admittance to the Mughal gardens would have been a restricted privilege, the literati of the city frequently participated in the *majlis* held in the gardens of the emperors and the *subedars*. Historians and hagiographers have recorded numerous anecdotes about these gatherings where sometimes the Mughal poet and his Kashmiri contemporary competed, sometimes even clashed, while satirizing each other.

Of the once numerous gardens in the city, four still remain, while the footprints of two more, Char Chinari and Bagh-i Saif Khan, are fast disappearing. The most famous are Shalimar Bagh, the site of the imperial court, and Chashma Shahi, a garden laid out by Shah Jahan around a spring. Both Shalimar and Chashma

Shahi are places of sedate calmness; they have a certain formality built into them—a space governed by courtly etiquette. Of all the Mughal gardens in Kashmir, Shalimar alone served as a miniature court, with its private and public audience hall, a symbol of the empire. Also surviving on the shore of the Dal is the garden of Nishat, a more vivid landscape, flamboyant in its autumn glory of blazing chinar trees, with rapidly ascending terraces. For me, it is a personal favourite. The open terraces of the garden (*tabkat* in Persian) were once interspersed with lofty wooden pavilions, *baradaris*, a design sourced from and modelled on the wooden porticos of the Safavids. An old painting of the *baradari* at Nishat looks remarkably similar to the entrance pavilion of Chehel Satoon in Isfahan. Long since demolished, these pavilions at Nishat provided a series of screened vistas both into the garden and the lake beyond. Constructed by Asaf Khan (d. 1641), Shah Jahan's vizier and father-in-law, Nishat has a famous story to it, widely reported in native histories. On a visit to Nishat, Shah Jahan found the garden too magnificent not to be in his possession, so he praised it lavishly. Court etiquette demanded that, given the emperor's praise, the vizier would offer it to him. But for once the vizier remained adamantly silent: the garden was too precious to be shared with his son-in-law and his master.

A short way beyond both Nishat Bagh and Chashma Shahi is a garden that was a collaborative project between Akhund Mulla Shah Badakshi and Shah Jahan's favourite children, Jahanara Begum and Dara Shikoh. This is Pari Mahal. Some say it was a spiritual retreat for the Sufi, constructed for him by the royal siblings, who were also his *murids* (disciples).

A major feature of the Mughal gardens is water. In the plains it is a shallow sheet of water moving slowly; in Kashmir, the water moves with force, in the water channels and down the cascades, with light flickering behind the water in arched

## CHIRAGAN (ILLUMINATION)

niches (*chinikhanas*). Illumination played a major part in how the garden was experienced. These *chinikhanas* were modelled on similar-looking niches in the royal apartment that held precious Chinese porcelain—a much-sought-after item in Muslim courts from Delhi to Isfahan. In the *baghs* of Kashmir, the last of the original *chinikhanas* at Shalimar, being badly damaged, were replaced with new ones, to mark a new celebration, Jashn-i Kashmir, a controversial concert in 2013 led by the Indian-born conductor and composer Zubin Mehta, and sponsored by the German Embassy.

So it was within this Mughal setting that in 1691 the Iranian visitor Husayn Sabzwari decided to sponsor an unusual event. He asked the men in his entourage to illuminate the foothills overlooking the lake. This must have been a great spectacle for Dedhmari to remember and record it in his history almost a century later, though his account is tempered with a degree of puritanical outrage. However, he does manage to confuse us with the details. For some unexplained reason, Dedhmari believed the illumination was a daytime event, which makes no sense. On the day of the illumination, Dedhmari writes: "To witness the celebrations on this occasion, a majority of the city dwellers with the purpose of picnicking took to boats [in the direction of the illumination]. The crowd on the boat kept on increasing ..."[1]

The Iranians were used to illuminating homes and shrines on major religious occasions; these included both Shab-i Qadr in the month of Ramzan, and Shab-i Barat.[2] Illumination and celebration on Shab-i Barat were also a tradition observed at the Mughal court. As Annemarie Schimmel puts it in *The Empire of the Great Mughals*, celebrations on Shab-i Barat at the Mughal court with "illuminations and fireworks" reflected Persianate cultural influences, which the Mughal emperors inherited from and shared with their counterparts in Persia.[3] Jahangir writes about such an event hosted by Nur Jahan in her garden: "the

14th of Shaabān, which is Shāb-i Barāt, I held a meeting in one of the houses of the palace of Nur Jahan Begum, which is situated in the midst of large tanks [...] In the beginning of the evening, they lit lanterns and lamps all around the tanks and building, [...] the like of which has perhaps never been arranged in any place."[4]

The practice of visiting graveyards and illuminating tombstones by lighting candles is a Mughal tradition that persists in the city, though, like many old customs and rituals, it is a dying one. The custom of illumination—*chiragan*—was not new to the Kashmiri landscape. It predates the arrival of both the Mughals and Islam. Jahangir refers to a Hindu festival held at Srinagar, with houses on both banks of the Jhelum illuminated with lamps. The illumination marked the ancient pre-Muslim Hindu festival of Kashmir called Vyeth Truwah (The Thirteenth of Vyeth, in Kashmiri), which celebrates the origin of the river Jhelum (Vyeth) on the thirteenth of the month of Bahdawan (August to September) in the Hindu calendar. Earlier, during Shahmiri rule, Zain al-Abidin also took to a boat to enjoy the festivities associated with the event.

Fast-forward two centuries and we find another *chiragan* happening in the city, the Diamond Jubilee Celebration held in the summer of 1897 to mark the sixtieth anniversary of Queen Victoria's accession to the throne. The maharaja's court had issued a direction to everyone in the city to illuminate their homes from 21 to 22 June, as the historian Munshi Hasan Ali records in his *Tarikh-i Kashmir*:

> On the hills, and in the city, and villages, illumination was done, and the city dwellers were also ordered as far as possible to light their homes and poor hovels. Consequently, the city dwellers by force or free will, from the poor to the rich, each according to his status, kept the equipment of illumination. In short, the illumination of the hills on one

side, the illumination of the city dwellers on one side, the royal illumination, and the bursting of firecrackers on one side—it was a unique celebration the likes of which Kashmir had never seen before.[5]

This was not to be the last *chiragan* in the city. A few years after the Jubilee celebration, Queen Victoria died, and her son Edward VII was proclaimed as the King-Emperor of Hindustan (*Qaisar-i Hind*) at the famous Delhi Durbar of 1903. An occasion of great pomp and festivity, the event was hosted in a tented city, carefully planned and curated by the Viceroy, Lord Curzon. Of the various modern conveniences provided to the assembled guests—the maharajas, rajas and nawabs—the one that stood out as a symbol of pomp and splendour was electric light. To an observer, the site of the Durbar resembled a finely "illuminated canvas city".[6] To mark the occasion, a special Delhi Durbar Medal was struck in gold and silver, bearing an inscription in Persian. The gold medals were awarded to the assembled native royalty. The design of the Persian inscription on the medal was undertaken by a Kashmiri calligrapher, Munshi Husayn Ali (d. 1933).[7] In the Munshi family archives at Srinagar, there is a letter of appreciation from the British Resident, conveying the Viceroy's admiration for Husayn Ali's work and a reward of fifty rupees. In the Durbar, though, the camp of the ruler of Kashmir, Maharaja Pratap Singh, stood out for the illumination provided by numerous light bulbs powered by a diesel generator, which Pratap Singh had brought to Srinagar for lighting the royal palace. As this wonder indicated, the nature of illumination in the city was about to change. The flickering lights of numerous candles would soon be replaced by the modern invention of electricity.

Soon the experiment was repeated in Srinagar, with the commissioning of the Mohra Hydroelectric power plant in 1908. Along with the royal palace at Sherghari and the house of the

British Resident, the main recipient of electricity was the silk factory on the city outskirts at Haft Chinar. The factory was a major investment for the local *durbar*, and many in the city found work there, though it was poorly paid. By the start of 1920, most of the street lamps in the city, from the royal palace to the heart of the city at Zaina Kadal, were running on electricity, replacing older kerosene spirit lamps. On his accession, Maharaja Hari Singh had the Mughal *baghs* in the city provided with electric lamps. These gardens, especially Shalimar, served as the site of evening tea parties for visiting colonial officials, including the Viceroy. And, as the maharaja, his court and their guests engaged in their parties under the *chinar* at Shalimar and Kothi Bagh and the Residency Garden, a labour protest erupted in the silk factory in 1924. Soon, the city would get drawn into the political upheaval that was shaking the foundations of the British Raj all over South Asia. The revolt had been brewing for some. Already in 1907, Munshi Hasan Ali had written: "There is no doubt that in all the land of Hindustan [India], for a few years, the fire of revolt is brimming, and people are becoming independent, and between the English and the Indian hate for each other is growing. And truth be said, the English people of today are not the same as the English of the past, and the Indians have also become [illegible]. The Bengalis have also taken to revolt."[8]

Kashmir would change, and so would Srinagar. In 1947, the British left India. There were popular revolts in Poonch and in Gilgit-Skardu against the maharaja. In the city the mood was politically charged, but there was no clarity on the emerging future; communalism was pulling the city towards alternative visions. A tribal force from the frontier regions of the newly established state of Pakistan would invade the territory of the maharaja, who, in panic, would flee, leaving the palace and the capital. The tribals (*kabail* in Kashmiri) would reach the city outskirts before being stopped by the Indian Army. Srinagar

## CHIRAGAN (ILLUMINATION)

and most of the former princely state of Jammu and Kashmir would become part of India. This annexation would be disputed by Pakistan, and a conflict would begin—the Kashmir dispute—which would result in two wars, a UN resolution, a bilateral agreement, and much more.

And, in the background of all this turmoil, the tradition of *chiragan* would continue. After all, it was also a means of celebration and, more importantly, a means to impress people. And in the winter of 1955, those in power in Srinagar outdid both the Dogra maharaja and the Mughal padshah in the scale of their festivities. For two days, on 9 and 10 December, the city hosted two leaders from the Soviet Union, Nikita Khrushchev and Marshal Bulganin. They would be taken out in a riverine procession on the Jhelum and feted on the banks of Dal Lake. On the shores of the lake, especially the Boulevard—the promenade—in between the occasional street lights, stood row upon row of candles, lit in a spectacle that has not been repeated since. The maharaja had been outdone. The *chiragan* put up for a communist had far outdone that given almost half a century earlier for an imperialist. The city people who were part of both events could say with some justification that their participation in these performances was enforced.[9] Nonetheless, they enjoyed it!

20

CHAI

> *In my previous china*
> *I brewed tea for you*
> *Come drink with me*
> *I can't get over you!*
>
> Mahmud Ghami (1765–1855),
> Sufi poet

THERE ARE THREE PROPS that by themselves are enough to represent life in Kashmir: a *kangir* (firepot), a *pheran* (long, loose outer tunic), and a samovar. The first two are essentials of life; they provide much-needed warmth and comfort during the winter. The samovar (Kashmiri: samavar) is where the Kashmiri allows himself some latitude in turning the pursuit of pleasure into an act of commonplace daily life. In Kashmiri society, the samovar has been effortlessly transformed from an object of luxury into something utilitarian.

For those familiar with Srinagar and how the city behaves, the poet Mahmud Gami's invitation to drink tea symbolizes the starting point of *suhbat* (companionship). Unlike in some Eastern cultures where sharing tea is seen as a ritual, a performance involving precise movements and pauses, in Srinagar sharing a cup of tea is an act devoid of any ceremony. Yes, there are a few nuances that, in the past, had indicated how cultured you were perceived to be, but these were not stringent rules. If you slurped while sipping your tea, that might be considered an unforgivable faux pas. But in a different setting, the same thing would be viewed as an act of enjoyment, indicating a sensory and attitudinal pleasure. To the host, it was a hint that the tea was good: pour some more! Some drinkers would turn over the handleless cups after taking the tea, in a sign they had finished. Others would indicate this verbally or by placing their hand flat over the cup. Depending upon how familial or formal the company was, you might empty the entire cup or leave a few drags to show you had had enough.

Today, the traditional chai—*nun-chai* (salty tea)—is brewed in a samovar, which everyone seems to agree is a Russian invention of the eighteenth century. Unlike the Russian samovar, which has an urn-like brass shape, Kashmiri samovars are made of copper. The shape borrows from the graceful curvilinear form of the *aftab* (ewer). The city museum has several copper samovars, mostly from the nineteenth century, their surfaces decorated with fine arabesque (*islim*). Porcelain cups—the china of Ghami was much valued—known as *finjan*, were mostly imported from Yarkand and Kashgar in Chinese Turkistan. Equally prized was the jade cup (*zahar mohar*), which a few of the city's wealthy merchants, with their transregional trade links, would source from the bazaars in Yarkand. Most people in the city survived on *koshur pyaleh*, a locally made coarse cup with a thick rim. Broken cups would be mended and reused—a group of artisans (*weatghar*) would perform this task. Some people in the city would refuse to sip tea from a mended cup or a cup with cracks, as it was seen as an inauspicious sign. Others would consider drinking from such a cup an act of humility, and cultivate it as a habit. Slowly the Yarkand market was replaced by Calcutta, and porcelain cups made in Europe and India found their way into the town. The Kashmiri Hindus were in the habit of taking tea in brass cups (*khous*), and when stainless steel arrived in the market, cups were made from this material. The Muslims, however, avoided drinking from metal cups.

# CHAI

In the heart of the city, near Zaina Kadal, stands an abandoned *kouth* known as Jafar Khan *sunz kouth*.[1] Jafar Khan was a wealthy Afghan pearl merchant who made his way to Srinagar somewhere towards the end of the nineteenth century. In the city, he diversified his trade, formed matrimonial links with Kashmiri families, and went on a spree buying valuable "real estate". This also included the *kouth* at Zaina Kadal, the property of the prominent Khwaja Mohyi al-Din Gandru. The *khwaja* had been a leading shawl merchant, but after his death, the family fell on hard times and were forced to sell the *kouth*. Jafar Khan, it seems, was more interested in a pile of Persian carpets stored in the house, so he bought the property lock, stock and barrel. Unfortunately, when the door to the house was opened, the Afghan merchant found all the carpets frayed beyond repair. According to city legend, the only valuable item he could find intact was a Victorian tea set.

So when did the city get its first taste of tea? Many merchant families claim that their ancestors introduced tea to Kashmir. There is no way of determining who and when, but it is likely that the merchant caravans that left for Central Asia introduced this custom to Kashmir. The Yarkandi *finjan* and the Russian samovar favour the Central Asian connection. When did this happen? Again, we have no definite answer. But, in the nineteenth century, we find several *masnavis* written in praise of chai. These *chai nama* (book of tea) indicate that taking chai had become an established custom in Kashmir in the nineteenth century. One of the *chai namas* was composed by Khwaja Shah Niyaz Naqshbandi (d. 1829), a merchant and master of a Sufi order with wide connections across Central Asia, from Kashgar to Bukhara. Ghami's offer to drink tea in a cup of fine china also supports the idea that in the nineteenth century, tea was the national drink of Srinagar and Kashmir.

The consumption and, more significantly, the enjoyment of tea were well established in the city, long before the advent of the British colonial administrators. The British, with their obsession with afternoon tea, did, however, lay the foundation for the practice of holding tea parties, soon to be imitated by the native court and all those Anglophiles whose careers revolved around the court. The initial British soirées were enacted in the *baghs* that the Mughals had built in the city. But the European affair in the garden proved to be a poor bureaucratic imitation that failed to compete with the scale and grandeur of the imperial Mughal *mehfil* (assembly). If they could have seen the spectacle, the Mughals would surely have marked it as a travesty, a sacrilege.

Teacups and saucers replaced the *finjan*, and in place of the samovar came the silver teapot, creamer and sugar bowl on a silver tray. Finger foods, cakes and biscuits, were served to the guests, sitting stiffly in their equally stiff wooden chairs. For the Kashmiri serving the guest, this version of chai—a mixture of milk, sugar and tea leaves brewed in hot water—must have seemed odd. Hardly any native in Srinagar knew about Thomas Lipton, his tea plantations in Ceylon or his penal labourers toiling in the foothills of the Himalayas to make this fine product. Soon Lipton chai became the only form of tea served to every high-ranking official on his arrival in Srinagar—a tradition Kashmiri officials follow even today.

In the city, all enjoyed tea. *Adab* demanded that you refrain from slurping your tea while drinking: it was, and still is, considered an uncouth, ill-mannered practice. Yet for the vast majority of people suffering the indignities of daily life, working as labourers on the street or toiling in the shabby, poorly ventilated hovels, this loud sound marked a certain fulfilment. It also made the tea taste better. Moreover, what was disdained in the city was welcomed with some relish in the countryside.

Both Muslims and Hindus enjoyed the same tea, and both claimed they only knew how to brew a perfect samovar of chai. But there were some subtle yet distinct differences, at least in drinking. A Hindu would usually hold the handleless cup in the long sleeve of his *pheran*, screening his hand from the heat of the tea. Not so for the Muslims.

While the traditional *chai* that most people in the city drank in the morning, at noon, and in the evening was (and, for some, remains) *nun-chai*, there was also the *kahwa*, the *sheer chai* and the *Mughal chai*, catering to different taste buds. Under British influence, Lipton tea became common, and people would take it in the morning and *nun-chai* at noon and in the evening. The British also started the tradition of high tea, although few locals were invited to these parties of tea, biscuits and cakes. Members of the native court also followed this tradition, organizing lavish tea parties for visiting colonial officers or on the birthday of the maharaja.

Somewhere in the twentieth century, a local baker was sent by the maharaja to Europe to be trained in the art of making cakes and biscuits. His bakery, now a hotel, The Ahdoos, is one of the most popular addresses for visitors to the city.

# 21

# AN IRANIAN LADY IN THE CITY

HER NAME WAS ZUHRA Bibi: as a child I would call her Bibi. Once a year, before or after Eid, she would arrive at our home to collect the *fitr*, the obligatory charity that Muslims must pay in the month of Ramzan before the festival. From what I recollect, she was a frail, bespectacled old lady of small stature with a face marked by countless wrinkles and, I think, grey eyes. Her life, from what I could understand as a child, was one of sadness and unending loss. She had lost her husband, her son and son-in-law, and was living in a rented house in the Abi Guzar neighbourhood of the city, with her many daughters, one of whom suffered from a disability, and with the children of her widowed daughter. Given her financial constraints, she would often change her rented accommodation. Despite her troubled life, she exuded a certain grace. Her demeanour was willow-like, bent and drooping yet supple in the face of adversity, as if still looking for change in her life. Did she bear life a grudge? Who knows. I asked my mother this question repeatedly, but she did not think so. She remembers Bibi as a person of stoic acceptance (*raza*), acquiescing in what destiny had served her. In traditional Muslim societies, *raza* embodies a state of contentment, of acceptance. Some Sufi treatises define *raza* as the highest state of human attainment.

Unlike many women of her age, Zuhra Bibi did not wear a *burka*. A long white *malmal chaddar* (linen head scarf) would cover her head and most of her upper body, as I vaguely recall. For someone who, even at an old age, had to toil from morning to evening to make ends meet, her white chintz dress would be amazingly spotless. Occasionally, she would dress in white satin with floral prints, though at that age I hardly knew the difference between the two. These would be gifts from her benefactors, often the clothes of someone who had died recently. It was a custom in the city that the clothes of the deceased would be distributed among the children. In the case of a male, the *dussa* (long male pashmina shawl), sword and Quran would be passed on to the eldest son, while the rest of his belongings would be distributed among the surviving siblings. Sometimes the son, daughter or daughter-in-law would simply refuse to share, and then for weeks, the *mohalla* would be full of rumours, of stories of human wickedness, greed and wrongdoing. If the clothes did not fit, then they would be gifted to someone who was seen as deserving and in need but also, more importantly, pious. For the bereaved family, the hope was that, in return, the receiver would pray for the departed soul. The Kashmiri Pandits probably also had a similar custom. This must have been a tradition that was established in the distant past when the city was relatively wealthy. Still, as with many other customs in the city, it was followed by families who could afford it.

What fascinated me most about Zuhra Bibi was her Persian. Apparently, she was of Iranian origin, and during the mayhem of the Partition the family had been somehow left stranded in Kashmir. I realize this cannot be her entire story, but then there is no one who can fill the gaps in Bibi's life. She could hardly converse in Kashmiri, though in all probability she understood it. Her conversation was always in Urdu. She would speak softly; her voice had a peculiar sweet flavour, unlike anything Kashmiri. But it was her Persian that I recall: sweet, melodious Persian. I would always pester her to speak a few sentences, and with a smile she would oblige. She would never frown or refuse. Sometimes she would recite a verse or two of Hafiz or Saadi and then explain the meaning in Urdu. These were lessons in life that the kid in me hardly understood. I simply loved to listen.

## AN IRANIAN LADY IN THE CITY

Despite all the troubles in her life, she remained an affectionate person, never asking for any help. Though the select few families in the city she visited would help her, this could hardly have been enough to meet her needs. The daughters were, I think, engaged in *sozini* craft—the exquisite embroidery that has made the Kashmiri shawl so famous. The last time I saw her was perhaps in 1988, before the insurgency broke out in Kashmir. Then, as trouble engulfed the city, disrupting daily lives, we forgot about her as all of us tried to cope with a changed life and a city increasingly disconnected from itself. Initially, for a few years my mother would wait for her arrival in the month of Ramzan, but she never came. We never saw her again. I am reminded of a half-verse of Hafiz, which could well have been Bibi's epitaph, if we only knew where she was buried: "Death is a favour to us."

In the city, death, like weddings, was and still continues to be a major event. Though a commemoration, it could and often did take the form of a public spectacle. Entire *mohallas* would be involved in both the funeral ceremony and the four-day mourning period culminating in the *rasm-i kul* or, as it is more commonly referred to, *fathiya*. A death such as Zuhra Bibi's, lost as it was in obscurity, was generally unheard of. The city had a term for such a lonely and unmourned death: *musafir marg*. The term, or rather the compound, is made of two Persian words. While *marg* simply signifies death, *musafir* has a more layered meaning. It was, and still is, used both for a traveller and for a pauper or mendicant, these days mostly for a street beggar.

During the eighteenth and nineteenth centuries, when many foreign merchants trading in the famed Kashmiri shawl arrived in the city, their presence in Srinagar gave rise to an unique urban typology: *musafir mazar*. These public graveyards, some of which still survive in the city, were endowed by foreign merchants for the purpose of burying those from their fraternity who never made it back home. Interestingly, while these shawl merchants hailed from a variety of nationalities, including Turkish, Armenian and Georgian as well as from mainland South Asia, a significant majority belonged to Iran—Zuhra Bibi's land. In the early part of the nineteenth century, around 300 of these Iranian merchants were based in Srinagar, adding to the cosmopolitan character of the city. In the city, within the neighbourhoods of Madin Saheb, Zadibal and Hassanabad, we find a few cenotaphs with inscriptions in Persian, the only surviving material evidence of this foreign mercantile presence in the city. Recently, in 2020 the British auction house of Sotheby's sold a complete Quran codex, written in Kashmir in 1246 AH / 1831 CE, for a whopping £7,016,250. The Quran had been commissioned by an Iranian merchant, Muhammad Ismai'l, who was identified in the codex as *tajir-al Isfahani*—the merchant from Isfahan.

While most of these Iranian merchants left Srinagar, after a severe incident of rioting in the city that took place in the early 1830s, a few did linger well into the last quarter of the nineteenth century. A rather colourful figure from this fraternity, and probably the last merchant of whom we have some details, was a resident of the Iranian shrine city of Mashhad, Hajji Abid. The merchant seems to have been much favoured at the court of Maharaja Gulab Singh, the first Dogra ruler of Kashmir. But then sometime in the third quarter of the nineteenth century, Hajji Abid had to flee Kashmir after losing a large part of his fortune. A native Kashmiri poet, Mahdah Shah Deykah, in his Persian *qasida* on the elite of the city, *Rayisnama-i Kashmir*, portrays the merchant, in spite of his title of "hajji", as a womanizer, who lost his fortune because of his apparent debauchery. On the other hand there are archival records which document Abid's patronage of religious sites in Srinagar, before he vanishes from public memory altogether.

No one knows when the hajji passed away, or in which city or town. Like Zuhra Bibi, we have no account of his last days.

## AN IRANIAN LADY IN THE CITY

What about the merchant's family? Did they travel back to their homeland in Iran or did they become part of Srinagar—another family like Bibi's which became indigenized in the city; another layer added to this rich and diverse city. And thus a flamboyant nineteenth-century shawl merchant and a poor widow from the twentieth century, both of Iranian origin, in all probability lie buried in some nameless grave in a *musafir mazar* of Srinagar.

> Upon my grave when I die,
> No lamp shall burn nor jasmine be,
> No candle with unsteady flame,
> No bulbul chanting overhead
> Shall tell the world I am dead.[1]

# 22

## TANZ-O MIZAH (SATIRE)

THE CITY OR, RATHER, the older *mohallas* still retain a wicked sense of humour: street humour, or *tanz*. For a city that, in its social exchanges, is still characterized by a degree of civility and politeness, this street humour directed its shafts at social hierarchies and human egos. It still exists, free of all guile, particularly among the young. Middle-aged men join in too and, sometimes for a brief moment, even the elderly. Traditionally, this exchange operates from the *pendh*, the small wooden ledge of a shop. Early morning or late evening, men—and it was always men—would gather on the *pendh* and gossip. The conversation would weave a life of its own, moving from the *pendh* to the narrow *kocha* (lanes) and *gulli* of the city, from the *kocha* to the main intersections (the *chowk*), and then on to the bridge. Sometimes, in what could be seen as an irreverence, it also made its way into the *hammams* (bathhouses) of the city mosques, much to the annoyance of the more pious individuals in the assembly, who visited only to pray.

Apart from the city streets, *tanz* flourished in between small limited breaks in the *chaat-i hal* and the *karkhanas* of the shawl and carpet weavers, the wood carvers, embroiderers and papier mâché workers. For these countless poor, underpaid, overworked artisans, young and old alike, toiling in bleak, sombre and sometimes dingy workplaces from early morning till late evening, this shared humour was life-affirming, creating bonds of commonality and togetherness.

So was this humour a product of male misogyny? Decidedly so, for street ownership was all-male. Was it perceived as such? Perhaps, but, unlike what prevails in many other parts of North

India, this earthy humour was free of verbal abuse or sexual innuendo. It did seek to disparage and maybe even belittle the life that existed in the *diwan khanas* and *baithaks* (living quarters used for social gatherings) of the city elite, but seldom if ever was the intent to humiliate. For those who were at the receiving end, they could either ignore it or be brave enough to engage, though few if any chose to do so. The street wit was too intense: no one wanted to lose face. Sometimes, but not often, the humour also made its way into the assemblies of the rich and powerful in the city. For the rich, those who dictated what culture—*tehzib*—meant, ideal behaviour was judged by refinement of manner, a certain delicacy in speech (*tamiz*) and also a sense of fortitude, of maturity (*burut-bari*). But there were countless in the city who would lampoon the artificiality of this *tehzib*, and satirize it.

# 23

# NAR (FIRE)

HISTORICALLY, SRINAGAR HAS LOST a far greater part of its built heritage to fire than to any incident of war or conflict. Since its first construction in 1402, the main mosque of the city, Jamia Masjid, has been burned four times, and the principal Sufi shrine in the city, Khanqah-i Maula, thrice. In a city where, till the very recent past, houses, mosques, temples and shrines were primarily built of wood and a mixture of stone and brick masonry, the threat of fire was an ominous, ever-looming eventuality. The arrival of winter, especially the forty days of the severe cold season of *chillai kalan*, always portended a conflagration, big or small, in the neighbourhoods of the old city. To fight the severity of the winter, with temperatures looming at sub-zero level, all that the citizens had was the *kangri*, an earthen wicker-covered coal pot that men, women and children carried under their loose winter tunic (*pheran*). No one knows when the tradition of using a *kangri* originated, but there are references to it in medieval Sanskrit texts. Now, at least among the affluent in the city, it serves as a discarded symbol of past poverty remembered and eulogized but rejected in favour of modern comforts.

Some houses in the city had *hammams*, the Kashmiri version of a Turkish bathhouse, where the rich could keep themselves warm. A few mosques in the city were also endowed with a *hammam*. Men, children and, in certain cases, women would frequent these public *hammams* to take a bath during the winter, paying a nominal amount. For women, their day and their time in the *hammams* would be reserved, usually to once a week.

Not many homes possessed the *maet*, those large copper tanks that were used to store water and were heated by burning firewood. It was only in the 1970s and 1980s that the expensive copper tanks became popular, and their use in homes was seen as a necessity rather than a luxury. Cooking would mostly occur on the earthen hearth, with wood, burned cow dung or driftwood easily sourced from the river serving as firewood. While the few lucky ones with a large enough compound would store the firewood along with the coal in separate outhouses, many would simply stock it in the attic located under the roof. Generally, it was the firewood stored for the winter months that would spark the horror of a fire, razing entire *mohallas* and leaving them as smouldering ruins.

My own experience with a fire in the city occurred at the age of ten or eleven, in the winter of 1986. It was a harsh winter, with heavy snow, frozen water taps, and icicles hanging from the roof eaves like drawn spears threatening everyone who passed beneath them. We were in the process of moving out from our home, a four-storey brick and stone building that my grandfather had built sometime in the 1930s. Luckily, the disaster happened in the daytime. News of the fire spread like a loud cry—more like a wail. And before any firefighter could arrive, it was the *mohalla* that poured into the unkept compound of our neighbour. Buckets of snow were heaped on the burning fire. The women in a neighbour's house climbed up to their attic, and held out copies of the Quran towards the fire, weeping and wailing, imploring divine intervention. Luckily, their prayers were heard, and the fire was put out.

# 24

## TAJIRAN-I SHAHR

IN 1831, MULLA MAHDI Mujrim (d. 1273 AH / 1857 CE), one of the last major Kashmiri poets to compose in Persian, wrote his *Shahr-Ashub* (The City's Misfortune, or The City's Disturber). Within the South Asian context, *shahr-ashub* emerged as a poetic form that attained some popularity with the decline of Mughal authority. It is a cry of lament on the decay of a city. The imperial capital of Delhi, which witnessed blood, mayhem and sacking multiple times, was a particularly favourite setting for many Urdu poets when locating their *shahr-ashubs*. But the genre was not limited to any particular time or city; we have, for instance, a *shahr-ashub* written on famine in Agra.[1]

Historically, this genre owes its origin to Saifi Bukhari (d. 1503),[2] a Persian poet who was connected to the Timurid court of Sultan Husayn Bayqara.[3] The Mughal emperor Babur had a very poor opinion of Saifi. In *Baburnama* he dismisses the poor poet as a mediocrity who "revelled in his *mullah* status [...], was a bad drinker and a poor drunkard".[4] Like most literati of his times, Saifi was a man of diverse interests; his expertise encompassed an eclectic mix of subjects, including Persian prosody. In my extended family library is a manuscript of *Raisala-i Saifi*, a work in Persian on *ilm-i aruz* (the science of prosody). This is a copy, along with a brief *sharah* (commentary), of the original work of Saifi, written in 896 AH / 1490 CE. This manuscript was copied by an ancestor, Mulla Hakim Azim al-Din (1269 AH / 1852 CE), in Lahore in 1831 while he was serving as a physician at the court of Maharaja Ranjit Singh. Azim would return to Srinagar during the rule of Shaykh Ghulam Mohyi al-Din (1842–1845). Mohyi al-Din held Azim in high regard as the most "*mʿūtabar* [reliable], *danā* [prudent], and *fahmida* [intelligent]" individual at his court.⁵ And, in the nineteenth century, Srinagar, a city far from the land of his birth, Saifi continued to be celebrated in literary circles. Aside from Azim's copy, numerous other manuscripts of *Raisala-i Saifi* were copied in this period at Srinagar, some of which still survive.

A greater part of Mujrim's poetry is panegyric in nature, in praise of his patrons, past and present. Many accounts speak of him being a favoured poet at the courts of both Sikh *subedars* and the Dogra rulers Maharaja Gulab Singh and his son Ranbhir Singh. The immediate context of Mujrim's *shahr-ashub* was a mutiny in 1841 by Sikh soldiers against the *subedar* Mihan Singh (1834–1841), which resulted in the *subedar*'s murder. The valley had already been ravaged by earthquakes, cholera and famine in the previous years. Ten years earlier, under the rule of an indolent *subedar*, Behma Singh, the city was devastated in one of the worst sectarian riots in its history. A large number of Iranian shawl merchants in the city (some texts mention 300 of them) left the city, never to return. From his court in Lahore, Maharaja Ranjit Singh, alarmed at this exodus, commanded his ministers to lure the merchants back to the city. Their departure meant great loss, as the shawl trade was a major item of commerce for the city and a significant form of revenue for the maharaja.

Mujrim's composition thus marks a particularly grim moment in the city's history, one of devastation, combined with the absence of effective government that could arrest this decay. As a literary work, it also marks a rupture between what was written about Kashmir and the city a century earlier under the Mughals, when poets vied with one another to write odes in praise of the city and its numerous monuments and gardens. In Mujrim's *shahr-ashub*, the city is a bazaar, and its merchants (*tajirs*) are the cause of its ruin. In the very first verse, the poet complains:

> The corrupt of this city trade in pleasant appearances
> The traders of the age trade in damages and penalties
> All the merchants that I see in this town
> Know of only one profit in this market: loss!⁶

The poet then goes on to name and shame some of the traders of loss in the city, whose mansions were built on the toil and exploitation of the vast majority of the city's artisan community.

Some of the misgivings that are voiced in the *shahr-ashub* also find a more forceful echo in another poem, a *masnavi* in Persian written by Mahdah Shah Deykah (d. 1895 CE), who is remembered in anecdotal accounts as a poet of sharp wit and a bitter tongue. The poet was a confidant of many of the rich and famous in the city; he was a regular participant in the gatherings (*majlis*) held in the merchants' and the courtiers' mansions. In his *masnavi*, titled *Rayisnama-i Kashmir* (Book of the Wealthy Kashmiris), Mahdah Shah complains about how those whose cheerful sounds made the city beautiful are now silent, in a city that has fallen prey to birds of ill omen:

> The nightingale and the parrot are muffled and mute
> The hawk and the crow are thrilled and excited.
> ...
> The corrupt and the depraved thrive and prosper
> And the honest merchants suffer losses and deprivation.⁷

Giving voice to the city's censure, Mahdah Shah takes great pleasure in mocking the mighty in the city for their conceit, feigned piety, wrongdoing, and, occasionally, debauchery. Very few get a genuine line of praise.

Many years back, while in a conversation with a senior papier mâché artist, a *wasta*, I asked him about his early years in the craft. "They were painful" was his first reply, and then he opened up slowly, telling me about his life of working from morning till evening along with the women in the family at odd jobs. (The role of women and children in our crafts is rarely mentioned, their toil forgotten.) For the *wasta*, there was no nostalgia. You were broken into the craft. His complaint concerned those merchants and traders who in his words fleeced their workers. The *wasta* was decently wealthy when I talked to him, but none of his children had followed him in the craft. This is again a story that gets repeated across artisan families in the city; a tale not exactly one of horror but certainly of abhorrence for the craft.

The plight of the poor artisans, however, failed to register in the imaginations of our poets. The complaint that both Mujrim and Mahdah Shah raise is generic to urban decay, corruption and malpractice in the city, not a voice in support of the poor working-class artisans. In most of the historical texts written in the nineteenth century, the authors refer to the artisan with great disdain, as an *ajlaf* (vagabond) who causes mischief and harm in the city. Abused by the *durbar* and the owner of the workshop (*kar-khandar*), the artisan typically fled his home and his land. In 1887, 300 Kashmiri shawl weavers living in Meshhad, Iran, petitioned the British *chargé d'affaires* in Tehran for recognition as British subjects. The claim was forwarded to the Foreign Secretary of British India at Calcutta, who sent a telegram to the British Resident in Kashmir to enquire. During the investigation, it was revealed that during the famine of 1832 many Muslims had left Kashmir for Punjab, and possibly Iran, though no "communication was maintained with them". Across Punjab, at Lahore and Amritsar, many of those Kashmiri migrants settled down, probably hoping to return back home—a return that never took place.

The establishment of Sikh rule in 1819 resulted in the erosion of the old class of landed elites in the city—the *jagirdars*, some of whom owned *jagirs* (land grants) from the Mughal era. These old *jagirdar* families, mostly Muslim, had their lands confiscated, as all Kashmir became the sole property of the Lahore *durbar*.

## TAJIRAN-I SHAHR

The role of the *jagirdars* was taken up by the intrepid Kashmiri merchant, who presided over a network of patronage linking him to the city. Across the plains of South Asia, from the city of Peshawar to Lahore and Amritsar, at the court of the nawabs of Awadh, and in the *kothis* of the banking *seths* of Calcutta, the Kashmiri merchant made his way, selling his commodities, of which the most precious was his pashmina shawl. The Kashmiri merchants managed a large part of the silk market at Peshawar, while one of their number rose to the position of nawab of Decca. The nineteenth-century Kashmiri merchant was essentially a workshop owner (*kar-khandar*), who gradually came to occupy the space of foreign merchants, the Turks, Persians and Georgians, whose forays into the city became increasingly infrequent as the authority of native rulers collapsed, and a rigid colonial system came to occupy this area from Punjab to Calcutta.

In 1878, the city of Paris held its third world fair, the Exposition Universelle, drawing a record thirteen million people and exhibits from many countries, including British India. Among Indian exhibits, the Gold Medal was awarded to a merchant from the city, Hajji Mukhtar Shah Ashai, for his shawls. Earlier, colonial officials arriving in Srinagar record meeting "Muhkta Shah", the shawl merchant. In the award roll he is remembered as the head manufacturer for the maharaja. Merchants such as Mukhtar Shah increasingly came to represent the people of the city, especially the overwhelming Muslim majority, to both the Hindu court and colonial officials like the British Resident.

But this manifestation of mercantile wealth in civic projects across the city happened gradually over time. Initially, it found its way into the patronage of religious spaces. Funding repairs and rebuilding at major religious sites was not only an act of personal devotion and piety but a public declaration of arrival and wealth. It was an investment in one's self-image as an elder of the city and its benefactor. *Rais-al Tujjar* ( the lord of the merchants) was how many would refer to themselves. Slowly, this mercantile wealth also spread into welfare schemes, particularly during stressful times of famine, flood or fire. In his memoirs, Munshi Muhammad Ishaq writes about this mercantile philanthropy during a severe case of famine: "People would search for scraps of food from the drains and eat them. During these (testing) times Khwaja Sana-al Lah Shawl, son of Khwaja Said al-Din Shawl, and the Shaykh family of Amira Kadal organized public kitchens (*langar*)."[8]

Earlier, during similar occurrences, especially in the Mughal period, it was the imperial court that would organize such relief works. Shah Jahan entrusted the *subedar* of Kashmir with organizing four public soup kitchens (*ghulurkhanas*) in the city for the poor and the destitute during a famine. The *subedar*, Abu Turbat Khan, proved to be unequal to the task, and was dismissed from his post and recalled.

In 1924, the elders in the city forwarded a petition to the maharaja to redress their plight, voicing a demand for justice in the face of recent atrocities. The petition was signed by eleven individuals, of whom five were merchants or representatives of families whose prestige was located in mercantile wealth. The freedom struggle launched against the Hindu rulers of Kashmir by the Muslim majority would be located in a space owned and operated by the city elite: the religious, landed and mercantile leadership. Soon they would be joined by another group of people hailing from a similar family background: a group comprising youths educated in the schools and colleges that originated from the colonial system.

25

A CITY IN REVOLT

*Night and day, I still wander in those fields; those dreams*
*Those secret keepers, those friends, what do I say of those*
*sweet faces?*

A K Naaz, migrant Pandit poet

IN CONFLICTS, AND MORE so in an armed conflict, you generally don't take sides: simply put, you are part of a side. This is the first act of a tragedy in which participation is not an option; it is simply an act of life. Conflict does not create a rupture in a society or a city but simply exacerbates existing fissures, whether we acknowledge them or not. Sometimes, individuals living in the same streets may genuinely claim to be unaware of the discontent. So, when the bubble of contentment and peace does burst, you may cry out with genuine astonishment, "People have gone crazy, my dear."

So, why then did Srinagar unravel in 1989? On the surface, going into the summer of 1989, everything seemed fine; the city was gradually becoming wealthy, lulled into acedia. Tourism, a major industry in the city, was booming, and state investment in the infrastructure of the city was increasing. Those whose business was to make money were making money. Historically, the city's culture dictated that any display of wealth should be made with humility and modesty. Srinagar was never ostentatious in its display of wealth. The notion of *patih duvlati* (old money) dictated this behaviour. But gradually, the shackles of imposed restraint were loosened. As new money made its way into society, some people complained about corruption, the inefficiency of the government, and nepotism. But these were commonplace complaints that were being raised in many parts of India. There was nothing unique about the discontent in the city. There were no visible signs of distress, and people in the city generally looked happy and content—and, yes, some complained. Yet the happiness was an illusion hiding a deep resentment that was to break out in a rancorous dispute, simultaneously violent and euphoric. The autumn of 1989 leading into the winter marked a crossroads in Srinagar's history, where the city encountered divisions. Nothing would be the same again: neither the physical fabric of the city nor its functioning. Many lanes and countless lives would be laid waste. There is a Srinagar before 1989, and a Srinagar after: the two have nothing in common. While this may be seen as pure rhetorical exaggeration, for many it is the truth. Even the memories, the inherited memories of the year and the years that followed, have been compartmentalized into mutually competing and contradictory narratives.

In February 1989, the Soviet Union completed its military withdrawal from Afghanistan. This was seen as a victory for the Afghan *mujahidin*, who were supported by many among the Muslim community of Kashmir. On 9 November 1989, the Berlin Wall came down. Earlier in August, Solidarity had replaced the Communists in Poland. The change happening in faraway lands was slowly filtering into the city, and people were talking. Across the city, people tuned into their radios to listen to these events. The unbelievable had happened. The Soviet bloc, seen as India's supporter in the international arena, was crumbling.

And then the winter of 1989 happened, suddenly, abruptly. Those winter nights were ominous, harbingers of a change no one had dreamed of. For some, those cold nights would remain the most frightful, dreadful moments of their life; for countless more, they marked hope. The state collapsed. Every grudge, every complaint that had been airbrushed away, now surfaced.

## A CITY IN REVOLT

Across the alleys and streets, it seemed the whole of Srinagar had come out to demand and to celebrate *azadi* (freedom). It was a mass popular uprising that, in its initial days, felt like a revolution, but very soon morphed into an armed insurgency before winding down into anarchy.

Popular belief in Srinagar associates the rise of armed militancy in the region with the screening of two movies, *Rambo III* (1988), and *Lion of the Desert* (1981), a historical war film about the Libyan freedom fighter Umar Mukhtar, with the lead role played by Anthony Quinn. Both movies had a Muslim undertone: the Afghan *mujahidin* against the communist Soviet Union and a bearded elderly teacher of the Quran against Mussolini's fascists in Libya. Yet one of the first major diktats of the militants, those who had taken up arms and revolted against the state, banned all cinemas in the city. And so one day, in one fell swoop, they all ceased to function.

Slowly, as the winter of 1989 progressed, new realities emerged. In those early autumn days, the city rejoiced at what seemed like the end of the state and its authority. Then came a realization: this was not Kashmir in revolt, but Muslim Kashmir. Armed militancy arrived and, with it, killings. The Hindus left; they would never return. All those pretty streets in the old city where the two communities had met daily, fell quiet. Neighbours became strangers. *Teim drayi*, they left. *Teim cheil*, they fled. These half-framed lines capture a narrative of loss and the movement of a people from their homeland. They also capture what became a perpetual divide in the physical landscape of the city and how the people imagine this moment unfolded in the streets and the alleys. For a majority of the city's Muslim population, it marked a just revolt, a time of celebration and great joy. For the Hindus in the city, it was a period of indescribable pain and fear. What defined the city in these crucial months was the smallest common denominator that joined individual to individual, family to family: their religious identity. The idea of Srinagar as a cosmopolitan city fell apart. A city is much like its people: it has a presentable, cultured face with a dark underside. But there are those singular instances in history when the two are framed together, staring at and not away from one other. For Srinagar, this moment was the winter of 1989.

And as the city became ungovernable, the self-assured hubris among the governing class, the politicians and the bureaucrats, was shaken. The unimagined had happened, and as in revolts worldwide, the politicians who had ruled rather than governed Kashmir fled: to Jammu, Delhi or wherever refuge could be found. With the withdrawal of the state, the perception of power and who yields it changed. Power now belonged to those who controlled the streets. For more than a decade, governance in the city was to be contested between agencies of the state and those who voiced support for separatism.

And in between all this, the crackdown started. It was brutal, as the state sought to reclaim lost streets and lost spaces. Gone were the long marches and the festive mood associated with the initial mass uprising. Now they were replaced with killings, reprisals, turf wars and much more. The city represented a war-scape, with armed bunkers at every street corner. Life and movement were curtailed to officially sanctioned hours. As crackdowns intensified in the city, the mundane, human side of life was laid bare to strange, prying eyes. Every cupboard, every *almirah*, every locked trunk was exposed to strange hands. This was both a visual and a physical violation.

For the vast majority of people living in Srinagar, the 1990s was a period of near misses, when you somehow survived miraculously. As an outsider, if you talk to people, they will recount stories of relatives, friends, neighbours and acquaintances who did not survive. Death was always on the horizon. The 1990s was all about cheating death, prison and torture. There

## A CITY IN REVOLT

was more to come: many more killed, houses burned, streets despoiled, women molested, lives interrupted. At times, Srinagar seemed to resemble a Foucauldian panopticon, where everyone is under constant surveillance until the very act of being seen loses its meaning: it becomes commonplace. But then there were so many commonplace occurrences in city life, such as being abducted by those who were claiming to fight for freedom, and held for ransom. Freedom, after all, needs money. Other more grotesque events became an acceptable part of living. Sometime in the same dark 1990s, someone came up with a solution for killing those who were deemed informers: hang them by the drawstrings of their trousers. And so, countless men were killed in this manner. After life, even death was deprived of any semblance of dignity. Some said the city was paying a price for the beauty of its surroundings. It was a heavy price, which the city continues to pay.

Those who visit the city are often struck by the friendly nature of the people, but they also seem to be surprised by the absence of smiles on the street. Not that the city people avoid eye contact while out walking, or are unused to people-watching, or carry a sullen expression. It is just that a smile is often missing.

A friend once observed that the modern history of Kashmir is a tragedy. Perhaps, but what was a tragedy decades ago has rapidly turned into a farce. Long before the city was plunged into dissent, Rehman Rahi (1925–2023) wrote a complaint that invoked the legacy of the Greek teacher Socrates, a figure both revered and extensively referenced in Islamicate cultures. Depending on how you frame them, his verses may be recast either as an elegy or as a eulogy for the city:

> Mortals drop dead while pursuing life.
> Won't you die?
> Will you empty the chalice in silence?
> Not even a sigh?[1]

# NOTES

## 1. PRELUDE

1. This is something that Moloy Chatterjee, a professor of architecture at the School of Planning and Architecture, New Delhi, once said in a seminar on the City in India held in the fall of 1998.
2. Some read the name simply as "The City", believing the name is a corruption of the honorific "Shree". European visitors to the city in the nineteenth century popularized the name as "The City of the Sun".
3. Nīlakaṇṭha, Kṣemendra and Bhallaṭa, *Three Satires*, transl. Somadeva Vasudeva (New York: New York University Press, 2005), 18.
4. Author's translation from Hakim Habib-al Lah, *Kuliyat-i Hakim Habib-al Lah*, ed. MY Manzar and Anis Kazmi (Srinagar: J&K Academy of Art, Culture and Languages, 1981).
5. *Masnavi* is a popular genre in Persian literature, comprising rhyming couplets on a similar theme. The most popular *masnavi* remains that of Rumi. The practice of writing *masnavi* in Kashmiri became popular during the nineteenth century.
6. W. Moorcroft and G. Trebeck, *Travels in the Himalayan Provinces of Hindustan and the Punjab; in Ladakh and Kashmir, in Peshawar, Kabul, Kunduz, and Bokhara*, vol. 2 (reprint, Srinagar: Gulshan Books, 2000 [1841]), 275.

7. See Ebba Koch, "The Mughal Emperor as Solomon, Majnun and Orpheus, or, The Album as a Think Tank for Allegory", *Muqarnas*, vol. 27 (2010).
8. For the translation of the Chinese text on the paper, I am indebted to the following Twitter accounts: @lucadelpant, @Wencheng_11 and @Yizhongren.
9. Author's translation from Allama Iqbal, *Payam-i Mashriq* (Lahore: Kapoor Art Printing Works, 1946).

## 2. THE ONE WHO CONQUERED ALL

1. Lalitaditya's ascent to the throne was preceded by that of his two elder brothers; for details, see Kalhana, *Kalhana's Rajatarangini: A Chronicle of the Kings of Kashmir*, transl. MA Stein, vol. 1 (Srinagar: Gulshan Books, 2007).
2. See Dennis Twitchett and John F. Fairbank (eds.), *The Cambridge History of China*, vol. 3 (Cambridge: Cambridge University Press, 2008).
3. Also see Tansen Sen, "Kashmir, Tang China, and Muktapida Lalitaditya's Ascendancy over the Southern Hindukush Region", *Journal of Asian History*, vol. 38 (2004).
4. Ronald Inden, "Imperial Puranas: Kashmir as Vaisnava Center of the World', in Ronald Inden, Jonathan Walters and Daud Ali (eds.), *Querying the Medieval: Texts and the History of Practices in South Asia* (Oxford: Oxford University Press, 2000), 62.
5. Abhinavagupta, *Abhinavagupta's Sri Tantraloka and Other Works*, transl. Satya Prakash Singh and Swami Maheshvarannda (Delhi: Standard Publishers, 2015), 299.
6. J.L. Masson and M.V. Patwardhan, *Santarasa and Abhinavagupta's Philosophy of Aesthetics* (Poona: Bhandarkar Oriental Research Institute, 1969), 39.

## 3. THE CITY OF PRAVARA

1. Kalhana, *Rajatarangini*, 19.
2. R.C. Kak, *Ancient Monuments of Kashmir* (London: The India Society, 1933), 105–111.

3. Matthew Leveille, "Teaching through Devotion: The Poetics of Yasaskara's *Devistotra* and Premodern Kashmir" (BS thesis, University of Wisconsin-Stevens Point, 2011), 6.
4. Samuel Beal (ed. and trans.), *Si-Yu-Ki: Buddhist Records of the Western World, translated from the Chinese of Hiuen Tsiang (AD 629)*, vol. 1 (London: Trübner and Co., 1884), 148.
5. Hakim Sameer Hamdani, *The Syncretic Traditions of Islamic Religious Architecture of Kashmir (Early 14th–18th Century)* (New York: Routledge, 2021), 3.

## 4. MONGOLS AND TURKS

1. *Baharistan-i Shahi: A Chronicle of Mediaeval Kashmir*, transl. KN Pandita (Srinagar: Gulshan Books, 2013).
2. See W.M. Thackston (ed. and trans.), *Rashiduddin Fazlullah's Jami ut-Tawarikh: Compendium of Chronicles; A History of the Mongols, Part One* (Cambridge, MA: Harvard University Press, 1998).
3. Ibid, 49.
4. Ibid, 478.
5. Ibid, 324.
6. *Baharistan-i Shahi*, 15.
7. Haider Malik Chadurah, *History of Kashmir*, transl. Razia Bano (Delhi: Bhavna Prakashan, 1991), 38.
8. Didda's hold over power commenced immediately on the death of her husband, Ksemagupta (r. 950–958), but after the death of her grandson Bhimagupta (r. 975–980), she ascended the throne in 980. See, Kalhana, *Rajatarangini*, vol. 1, 262.
9. Ibid.
10. Ibid.
11. The entire episode becomes somewhat farcical when we remember that the texts depicting the queen's suicide are based on Persian histories written by Muslim historians.
12. Following the Shahmiris, The Chaks on assuming kingship would also initially follow this tradition. For an account of the Chak rule, see Chadurah, *History of Kashmir*.

## 5. SHAHR-I KASHMIR

1. Even earlier, Brahmin families of Gandhara who had been settled in Kashmir by Mirkhula were banished by King Gopaditya and replaced by more orthodox Brahmins to root out any trace of non-Vedic Hinduism. See, Kalhana, *Rajatarangini*.
2. This corresponds to the year 1444 CE.
3. Chadurah, *History of Kashmir*, 52.

## 6. KHANQAH-I MAULA

1. Sayyid Ali, *Tarikh-i Kashmir*, transl. Ghulam Rasul Bhat (Srinagar: Center of Central Asian Studies, 1994).
2. Hakim Sameer Hamdani, *Shi'ism in Kashmir* (London: IB Tauris, 2023).
3. *A Study of Surviving Architectural Epigraphy in Kashmir from 16th–19th Century CE* (unpublished report, The Barakat Trust, 2023).

## 7. NAU SHAHR

1. Jonaraja, *Kingship in Kashmir (AD 1148–1459), From the Pen of Jonaraja, Court Pandit to Sultan Zayn al-Abidin*, transl. Walter Slaje (Halle: Universitätsverlag Halle-Wittenberg, 2014), 227.
2. Haidar Mirza, *The Tarikh-i-Rashidi of Mirza Muhammad Haidar, Dughlat: A History of the Moghuls of Central Asia*, transl. E. Denison Ross, ed. N. Elias (London: Curzon Press, 1972 [1895]), 429.
3. Ibid.

## 8. JAMIA-I SRINAGAR

1. See W.M. Thackston (ed. and trans.), *The Jahangirnama: Memoirs of Jahangir, Emperor of India* (Oxford: Oxford University Press, 1999).
2. See *Baharistan-i Shahi*, 39.
3. Wheeler Thackston, email to author, 2024.

## 9. DUMATH

1. *A Study of Surviving Architectural Epigraphy in Kashmir from 16th–19th Century CE.*

## 10. A MUGHAL EMPEROR IN THE CITY

1. See Sunil Sharma, *Mughal Arcadia: Persian Literature in an Indian Court* (Cambridge, MA: Harvard University Press, 2017).
2. His original name was Mulla Shafia and he belonged to the Iranian city of Yazd. See H. Beveridge et al., *The Maathir-ul-Umara, Being Biographies of the Muhammadan and Hindu Officers of the Timurid Sovereigns of India from 1500 to about 1780 AD*, revised by Baini Prashad (Patna: Janaki Prakashan, 1979), 446. Bernier records his trip having taken place in 1664.
3. Muhammad Salih Kambo, *Amal-i Salih*, transl. N. Hasan Zaidi (Lahore: Urdu Science Board, 2004), vol. 2, 27.
4. See Thackston, *The Jahangirnama*,
5. The folio is located in Maulana Azad Library, Aligarh Muslim University, Aligarh.
6. Thackston, *The Jahangirnama*, 335.
7. Murad Khan Mumtaz, *Faces of God: Images of Devotion in Indo-Muslim Paintings, 1500–1800* (Leiden: Brill, 2023), 248.
8. François Bernier, *Travels in the Mogul Empire, AD 1656–1668* (Oxford: Oxford University Press, 1916), 2.
9. See Kambo, *Amal-i Salih*.

## 11. MAZAR-I SHOURA

1. Translation, Mehran Qureshi.
2. Muzafar Alam, "Persian in Precolonial Hindustan", in Sheldon Pollock (ed.), *Literary Cultures in History: Reconstruction from South Asia* (Berkeley, CA: University of California Press, 2003), 160.
3. Ghani Kashmiri, *The Captured Gazelle: The Poems of Ghani Kashmiri*, transl. Mufti Mudasir Farooqi and Nusrat Bazaz (New Delhi: Penguin, 2013), xxiii.

## 12. RAGHUNATH MANDIR

1. *A Study of Surviving Architectural Epigraphy in Kashmir from 16th–19th Century CE.*

## 13. THE BUND

1. P.S. Nazaroff, *Moved On! From Kashgar to Kashmir* (London: George Allen and Unwin, 1935), 299.
2. H.W. Bellew, *Kashmir and Kashghar: A Narrative of the Journey of the Embassy to Kashghar in 1873–74* (London: Trübner and Co., 1875), 64.

## 14. CITY ON A MAP

1. In conversation with M. Saleem Beg, who served as the director general of tourism in 2002–2006.
2. Susan Gole, *Indian Maps and Plans, from earliest times to the advent of European surveys* (New Delhi: Manohar, 1989).
3. Gole indicates four bridges, but my impression is that five bridges are clearly marked. These would be Zaina Kadal, Fateh Kadal, Habba Kadal, Aali Kadal and Safa Kadal. Amira Kadal and Nawa Kadal both date to the Afghan rule, and thus are missing on a Mughal map. See Susan Gole, *Indian Maps and Plans: From Earliest Times to the Advent of European Surveys* (Delhi: Manohar Publications, 1989).

## 15. AN ASSEMBLY OF POETS

1. These walls are also known as *machey dous* (earthen wall) or *yandiri dous* (spindle wall).
2. Nautch is a corruption of the Hindustani word *natch* (dance).
3. Mohammad Ishaq Khan, *History of Srinagar, 1846–1947: A Study in Socio-cultural Change* (Delhi: Cosmos Publications, 1999), 104–105.

## 17. THE BAGH (GARDEN)

1. Under the Sikhs, the government took seventh-eighths of any crop from fields near the city.

2. Amir Khan's rule is celebrated in a *masnavi* written by a poet from the city, Munshi Muhammad Baqi. Baqi's father, Mulla Sateh, was also a poet favoured by the Mughal emperor Farrukhsiyar (r. 1713–1719).
3. George Forster, *A Journey from Bengal to England through the Northern Part of India, Kashmire, Afghanistan, and Persia, and into Russia by the Caspian Sea*, vol. 2 (London: R Faulder, 1798), 15–16.
4. Victor Jacquemont, *Letters from India*, vol. 2 (London: Edward Churton, 1834), 110.
5. Moorcroft and Trebeck, *Travels in the Himalayan Provinces*, 120.
6. Sir Francis Younghusband and Major E Molyneux, *Kashmir, Described by Sir Francis Younghusband, Painted by Major E Molyneux* (London: Adam and Charles Black, 1911), 81.

## 18. SAEER (OUTING)

1. 21 March, the Persian New Year.
2. I have observed it on many occasions while travelling through North Kashmir, especially in the village of Sadarkote.
3. Ghani Kashmiri, *The Captured Gazelle*, 201–207.
4. The fort was again briefly besieged by Shaykh Imam al-Din, the last Sikh *subedar* of Kashmir, but again the standoff ended without a battle.
5. A spring festival popular in North India, especially among the Sikh community. It usually falls on 13 or 14 April.

## 19. CHIRAGAN (ILLUMINATION)

1. Khwaja Muhammad Azam, *Vakat-i Kashmir*, transl. Shams-ud-Din Ahmad (Srinagar: Jammu and Kashmir Islamic Research Centre, 2001), 320.
2. Shab-i Qadr occurs in the ninth month of the Islamic calendar, while Shab-i Bara is celebrated a month earlier in Shaban.
3. Annemarie Schimmel, *The Empire of the Great Mughals: History, Art and Culture* (London: Reaktion Books, 2004), 138.

4. Thackston, *The Jahangirnama*, 385.
5. Munshi Hasan Ali, *Tarikh-i Kashmir* (unpublished manuscript), entry for June 1896.
6. Leo Coleman, *A Moral Technology: Electrification as Political Ritual in New Delhi* (Ithaca, NY: Cornell University Press, 2017), 48.
7. Munshi Husayn Ali was the head Persian teacher at the State School, which had been set up in the erstwhile Mughal Garden, Bagh-i Dilawar Khan, Srinagar, and had succeeded his father in the post.
8. Ali, *Tarikh-i Kashmir*, entry for 14 May 1907.
9. Popular anecdotes speak about how prayers were not offered in many mosques of the city as a result of the procession.

## 20. CHAI

1. Kashmiri for *kothi*.

## 21. AN IRANIAN LADY IN THE CITY

1. Translation of a Persian verse from Pran Nevile, *Lahore: A Sentimental Journey* (Delhi: Penguin, 2006), xv.

## 24. TAJIRAN-I SHAHR

1. See V.B. Singh (ed.), *Economic History of India, 1857–1956* (Delhi: Allied Publishers, 2002).
2. That the *shahr ashub* did exist even before Saifi but mostly "in the form of unconnected rubais" is the view held by Sunil Sharma, interview with author, 2024.
3. See Sunil Sharma, "Shahrshub", in Ehsan Yarshater, *Persian Lyric Poetry in the Classical Era, 800–1500* (London: IB Tauris, 2019).
4. Stephen F. Dale, *Babur, Timurid Prince and Mughal Emperor, 1483–1530* (Cambridge: Cambridge University Press, 2018), 80.
5. Hamdani, *Shi'ism in Kashmir*, 78.
6. Ibid.

7. Translation by Mehran Qureshi.
8. Munshi Muhammad Ishaq, *Nida-i Ḥaq*, ed. Munshi Ghulam Ḥasan (Srinagar: Markaz-i Ishayat, 2014), 60.

## 25. A CITY IN REVOLT

1. Translation by Mehran Qureshi.

# BIBLIOGRAPHY

Abhinavagupta, *Abhinavagupta's Sri Tantraloka and Other Works*, transl. Satya Prakash Singh and Swami Maheshvarannda (Delhi: Standard Publishers, 2015).

Alam, Muzafar, "Persian in Precolonial Hindustan", in Sheldon Pollock (ed.), *Literary Cultures in History: Reconstruction from South Asia* (Berkeley, CA: University of California Press, 2003).

Ali, Munshi Hasan, *Tarikh-i Kashmir* (unpublished manuscript), personal collection, Dr Ifthikhar Munshi, Srinagar.

Ali, Sayyid, *Tarikh-i Kashmir*, transl. Ghulam Rasul Bhat (Srinagar: Center of Central Asian Studies, 1994).

Azam, Khwaja Muhammad, *Vakat-i Kashmir*, transl. Shams-ud-Din Ahmad (Srinagar: Jammu and Kashmir Islamic Research Centre, 2001).

*Baharistan-i Shahi: A Chronicle of Mediaeval Kashmir*, transl. K.N. Pandita (Srinagar: Gulshan Books, 2013).

Beal, Samuel (ed. and trans.), *Si-Yu-Ki: Buddhist Records of the Western World, translated from the Chinese of Hiuen Tsiang (AD 629)*, vol. 1 (London: Trübner and Co., 1884).

Bellow, H.W., *Kashmir and Kashghar: A Narrative of the Journey of the Embassy to Kashghar in 1873–74* (London: Trübner and Co.,1875).

Bernier, François, *Travels in the Mogul Empire, AD 1656–1668* (Oxford: Oxford University Press, 1916).

# BIBLIOGRAPHY

Beveridge, H. et al., *The Maathir-ul-Umara, Being Biographies of the Muhammadan and Hindu Officers of the Timurid Sovereigns of India from 1500 to about 1780 AD*, revised by Baini Prashad (Patna: Janaki Prakashan, 1979).

Chadurah, Haider Malik, *History of Kashmir*, transl. Razia Bano (Delhi: Bhavna Prakashan, 1991).

Coleman, Leo, *A Moral Technology: Electrification as Political Ritual in New Delhi* (Ithaca: Cornell University Press, 2017).

Dale, Stephen F. *Babur, Timurid Prince and Mughal Emperor, 1483–1530* (Cambridge: Cambridge University Press, 2018)

Forster, George, *A Journey from Bengal to England through the Northern Part of India, Kashmire, Afghanistan, and Persia, and into Russia by the Caspian Sea*, 2 vols. (London: R Faulder, 1798).

Ghani Kashmiri, *The Captured Gazelle: The Poems of Ghani Kashmiri*, transl. Mufti Mudasir Farooqi and Nusrat Bazaz (New Delhi: Penguin, 2013).

Gole, Susan, *Indian Maps and Plans: From Earliest Times to the Advent of European Surveys* (Delhi: Manohar Publications, 1989).

Habib-al Lah, Hakim, *Kuliyat-i Hakim Habib-al Lah*, ed. MY Manzar and Anis Kazmi (Srinagar: J&K Academy of Art, Culture and Languages, 1981).

Haidar Mirza, *The Tarikh-i-Rashidi of Mirza Muhammad Haidar, Dughlat: A History of the Moghuls of Central Asia*, transl. E Denison Ross, ed. N. Elias (London: Curzon Press, 1972 [1895]).

Hamdani, Hakim Sameer, *Shi'ism in Kashmir* (London: IB Tauris, 2023).

Hamdani, Hakim Sameer, *The Syncretic Traditions of Islamic Religious Architecture of Kashmir (Early 14th–18th Century)* (New York: Routledge, 2021).

Inden, Ronald, "Imperial Puranas: Kashmir as Vaisnava Center of the World', in Ronald Inden, Jonathan Walters and Daud Ali (eds.), *Querying the Medieval: Texts and the History of Practices in South Asia* (Oxford: Oxford University Press, 2000).

Iqbal, Allama, *Payam-i Mashriq* (Lahore: Kapoor Art Printing Works, 1946).

# BIBLIOGRAPHY

Ishaq, Munshi Muhammad, *Nida-i Ḥaq*, ed. Munshi Ghulam Ḥasan (Srinagar: Markaz-i Ishayat, 2014).

Jacquemont, Victor, *Letters from India*, 2 vols. (London: Edward Churton, 1834).

Jonaraja, *Kingship in Kashmir (AD 1148–1459), From the Pen of Jonaraja, Court Pandit to Sultan Zayn al-Abidin*, transl. Walter Slaje (Halle: Universitätsverlag Halle-Wittenberg, 2014).

Kak, R.C., *Ancient Monuments of Kashmir* (London: The India Society, 1933).

Kalhana, *Kalhana's Rajatarangini: A Chronicle of the Kings of Kashmir*, transl. M.A. Stein, vol. 1 (Srinagar: Gulshan Books, 2007).

Kambo, Muhammad Salih, *Amal-i Salih*, transl. N. Hasan Zaidi, 2 vols. (Lahore: Urdu Science Board, 2004).

Khan, Mohammad Ishaq, *History of Srinagar, 1846–1947: A Study in Socio-cultural Change* (Delhi: Cosmos Publications, 1999).

Koch, Ebba, "The Mughal Emperor as Solomon, Majnun and Orpheus, or, The Album as a Think Tank for Allegory", *Muqarnas*, vol. 27 (2010).

Leveille, Matthew, "Teaching through Devotion: The Poetics of Yasaskara's *Devistotra* and Premodern Kashmir" (BS thesis, University of Wisconsin-Stevens Point, 2011).

Masson, J.L. and M.V. Patwardhan, *Santarasa and Abhinavagupta's Philosophy of Aesthetics* (Poona: Bhandarkar Oriental Research Institute, 1969).

Moorcroft, W. and G. Trebeck, *Travels in the Himalayan Provinces of Hindustan and the Punjab; in Ladakh and Kashmir, in Peshawar, Kabul, Kunduz, and Bokhara*, vol. 2 (reprint, Srinagar: Gulshan Books, 2000 [1841]).

Mumtaz, Murad Khan, *Faces of God: Images of Devotion in Indo-Muslim Paintings, 1500–1800* (Leiden: Brill, 2023).

Nazaroff, S., *Moved On! From Kashgar to Kashmir* (London: George Allen and Unwin, 1935).

Nevile, Pran, *Lahore: A Sentimental Journey* (Delhi: Penguin, 2006).

Nīlakaṇṭha, Kṣemendra and Bhallaṭa, *Three Satires*, transl. Somadeva Vasudeva (New York: New York University Press, 2005).

# BIBLIOGRAPHY

Schimmel, Annemarie, *The Empire of the Great Mughals: History, Art and Culture* (London: Reaktion Books, 2004).

Sen, Tansen, "Kashmir, Tang China, and Muktapida Lalitaditya's Ascendancy over the Southern Hindukush Region", *Journal of Asian History*, vol. 38 (2004).

Sharma, Sunil, *Mughal Arcadia: Persian Literature in an Indian Court* (Cambridge, MA: Harvard University Press, 2017).

Singh, V.B. (ed.), *Economic History of India, 1857–1956* (Delhi: Allied Publishers, 2002).

*A Study of Surviving Architectural Epigraphy in Kashmir from 16th–19th Century CE* (unpublished report, The Barakat Trust, 2023).

Sufi, G.M.D., *Kashmir, Being a History of Kashmir from the Earliest Times to Our Own*, 2 vols. (Lahore: University of Punjab, 1949).

Thackston, W.M. (ed. and trans.), *Rashiduddin Fazlullah's Jami ut-Tawarikh: Compendium of Chronicles; A History of the Mongols, Part One* (Cambridge, MA: Harvard University Press, 1998).

Thackston, W.M. (ed. and trans.), *The Jahangirnama: Memoirs of Jahangir, Emperor of India* (Oxford: Oxford University Press, 1999).

Twitchett, Dennis and John F. Fairbank (eds.), *The Cambridge History of China*, vol. 3 (Cambridge: Cambridge University Press, 2008).

Vigne, G.T., *Travels in Kashmir, Ladak, Iskardo, the Countries Adjoining the Mountain-Course of the Indus, and the Himalaya, North of the Panjab*, vol. 1 (London: H Colburn, 1842).

Yarshater, Ehsan, *Persian Lyric Poetry in the Classical Era, 800–1500* (London: IB Tauris, 2019).

Younghusband, Sir Francis and Major E. Molyneux, *Kashmir, Described by Sir Francis Younghusband, Painted by Major E Molyneux* (London: Adam and Charles Black, 1911).

# INDEX

Aali Kadal, 62
Abbasid Caliphate, 22, 23, 51
Abdullah, Shaykh Muhammad, 182
*Abhidharma Mahavibhasa Sastra*, 39
Abhimanyu, King, 61
Abhinavagupta, 12, 26–7, 28
Abid, Hajji, 208
Afghanistan, 167, 230
Agra, 9, 80, 151, 221
Ahmad Ali, Mulla, 78
Ahsan, Nawab Zafar Khan, 109, 151–3, 167
Akbar, Emperor, 49, 80, 106, 110, 114, 123, 160
*Album of Kashmiri Trades*, 74–5
Alchi temples, 50–1, 94
Alexander, 22
Ali Shah, 85
Ali, Munshi Hasan, 180–1
Aligarh, 173
ambo III (1988) (movie), 231
Amherst College, 74

Amira Kadal, 134, 135, 137
Amritsar, 224, 225
Anandeshwar Temple, Maisuma, 128
*Ancient Monuments of Kashmir* (Kak), 38
Archaeological Survey of India, 25, 92
Ashai, Hajji Mukhtar Shah, 225
Ashoka, Emperor, 35, 37, 39
Attila the Hun, raids of, 42
Aurangzeb Alamgir, Muhi al-Din Muhammad, 92, 105–6, 111, 113, 114
    arrival in Srinagar, 109–10
Azim al-Din, Mulla Hakim, 221

Baba Bulbul (also, Bulbul Shah), 61, 62
Babur, Emperor, 86, 221
Bactria, 38
Badakshi, Akhund Mulla Shah, 112, 113, 188

# INDEX

Badami Bagh cantonment, 39–40, 42
Badamwari, 110
Badayuni, Fani, 21
Bagh (the Garden), 27–8, 110–11
Bagh-i Bahr Ara, 110–11
Bagh-i Faiz Baksh, 113
Bagh-i Nurafza, 110
*Baharistan-i Shahi*, 58, 59, 73, 92
Balkh, 167
Banaras, 9
Baramulla, 106
*bayid-i Majnun,* 166
Bayqara, Sultan Husayn, 221
Begampur Friday mosque, 93
Bellew, HW, 134
Bengal, 94, 142
Berlin Wall, 230
Bernier, François, 105, 106, 109, 114–15, 143
Bhimanayaka, 51
Bhimber, 106
Bibi, Zuhra, 205–9
Bihar, 142
Bijbehara Temple, 47
Bilhana, 45–6
boats, 106–7
Bodhisattva, 41
Bourne, Samuel, 155
Brahmins, 25, 43, 44
*Brhatkatha,* 48
British and map-making, 142
Buddhism, 2, 23, 34–5, 37, 39
Bukhari, Saifi, 221
Bukhari, Sayyid Qamar al-Din, 183
Bulbul Lanker, 62

Bulganin, Marshal, 193
The Bund, 135–6
Burke, John, 40

Calcutta, 198, 224, 225
Carpenter, William, 80–1, 107–8
cartography, 142
Ceylon, 200
*chai nama* (book of tea) (Shah and Naqshbandi), 199
Chaks, 64, 99, 160
Chandigarh, 10
Char Chinari, 183, 187
Chashma Shahi, 187–8
China, 23, 35–6
chini dous (Chinese wall), 153
Constantinople, 101
Corbusian architecture, 10
*Corpus of Sarada Inscriptions of Kashmir* (Deambi), 79
Council of Regency, 133
cross-culturalism, 13–14, 15
Curzon, Lord, 191

Dachigham-Telbal *nallah,* 37
*Daksinamurti,* 27–8
Dal Lake, 107, 108, 183, 187–8, 193
Damaras, 48
Dara Shikoh, 111, 112, 113–14
Deambi, BK, 79
Decca, 225
Dedhmar, 60, 61
Dedhmari, Khwaja Muhammad Azam, 76, 187, 189
Delhi Durbar Medal, 191
Delhi Durbar, 191

# INDEX

Delhi, 9, 80, 151, 221, 232
Devi Temple, Pokhribal, 128
*Devistotra* (Ratnakantha), 44
Deykah, Mahdah Shah, 208, 223
Didda, Queen, 60–1
al-Din Hamdani, Khwaja Rashid, 58–9, 73
al-Din Nakhshabi, Ziya, 48–9
al-Din, Shaykh Imam, 135
Dogra dynasty, 15, 40, 127, 128, 133
rulers, 174, 193
Drugjan, 121
Dughlat, Mirza Haidar, 86
Dumath (mausoleum), 100–1, 144
Durlabhaka (Pratapaditya), 21, 25

Edward VII, 191
Elias, Jamal, 77
*Empire of the Great Mughals, The* (Schimmel), 189
Europe, 198, 201
European visitors, 114–15, 133–6
Exposition Universelle, 225

*farman*, 109, 110
*Fate Written on Matchboxes, A* (Kanjwal), 183
Fateh Kadal, 136
Fateh, Shah Aboul, 122
Fauq, Munshi Muhammad Din, 119, 120, 121
Forster, George, 45, 179
forward defence policy, 23
Fourth Buddhist Council, Kundalavana, 39

Gadadhar Temple, 127–8
Gaggaka, 79
Gami, Mahmud, 197
Ganderbal, 183
Gandhara, 35, 38, 43, 46
  Brahmins of, 44
Gandru, Khwaja Mohyi al-Din, 199
Garuda (Hindu deity), 24
Ghami, 199
Ghani Kashmiri, Mulla Tahir, 123 181
Ghazan, Sultan, 58
Ghazi Shah Chak, Sultan 99
Ghulam Muhammad, Bakshi, 182–3
Gilgit-Baltistan, 23
Gilgit-Skardu, 192
Gole, Susan, 143, 144
Graeco-Bactrian kingdoms, 38
Great Revolt (1857), 142
Great Trigonometrical Survey, 142, 143
Green Line, 137
*Greist Nama* (Book of Village Life) (Habib, Kralawari), 12–13
Gulab Bhawan, 136
Gunavarman, monk, 36
Gupkar, 187
Gupta Empire, 2, 24–5, 43
Gur-i Amir, 100
Gwalior, 43

Habba Khatun, Queen, 67
Habib Shah, Sultan, 99
Habib-al Lah, Mulla Hakim, 12–13

251

# INDEX

Hafiz Nagma, 154–5
Haft Chinar, 192
Haider, Malik, 59, 68–9, 94
Hamdani, Mir Muhammad, 78, 79, 93
Hamdani, Mir Sayyid Ali (also, Shah Hamdan), 69, 74, 76–7
Hamza Makhdum, Shaykh, 159–60
Harsha, reign of, 47–8, 49, 50, 51, 52
Harwan, 37–8
Hasan Ali, Munshi, 190–1, 192
Hassanabad, 208
Hazratbal shrine, 183
Herat, 86, 167
*Hindu Rulers, Muslim Subjects* (Rai), 78
Hinduism, 2, 24–5, 43
Hindus, 76, 77–8, 129, 183, 201, 231–2
*History of Srinagar City* (Khan), 155
House of Gonanda, 42, 44
House of Lohara, 60, 61
Hulegu Khan, 58–9
Huns, 2, 42–4
Husayn Ali, Munshi, 191
Hyun Jin Kim, 42

Ibn Khaldun, 99
Ilkhanate court, 58, 73
imperial albums (*muraqqa nigari*), 15–16, 48–9, 108
Indian Army, 192
Iqbal, Allama, 17
Iraki, Mir Shams al-Din, 80

Iran, 68, 73, 167, 208, 224
Iranian shawl merchants, 222
Ireland, 151
Isfahan, 208
Ishaq, Munshi Muhammad, 226
Ismai'l, Muhammad, 208

Jacquemont, Victor, 170
Jahanara Begum, 111, 112, 113–14, 161, 188
Jahangir, Emperor, 47, 92, 94, 95, 108, 110, 115, 169, 189–90
  on boat of "Kashmiri design", 106
  garden, 165–75
Jahanpanah, 93
Jaipur Map, 143–5
*Jami al-Tawarikh*, 58, 73
Jamia Masjid, 154, 217
Jamia-i Khiva, 94
Jamia-i Srinagar, 91–9
  fire and reconstruction, 94–5
  four-*iwan* plan, 93
  construction, 94
  Shrivara on, 91–2
Jammu & Kashmir Bank, 110
Jammu, 127, 232
Jawan Sher, Amir Khan, 167–8
Jhelum Cart Road, 134
Jhelum river (Vitasta), 21, 33, 44, 45–6, 48, 62, 144, 168, 174, 181, 190
  boats, 106–7
"Jilwah-i Naz", 151
Jonaraja, Pandit, 57, 63, 86

Kabul, 44, 69, 152, 167, 182

# INDEX

Kak, Pandit Birbal, 78
Kak, Pandit Ram Chandra, 37–8
Kalhana, 21–3, 26, 28, 35, 37, 42, 43, 45, 47, 49, 60, 61
Kamalashri, monk, 58
Kambo, Muhammad Salih, 115
Kandahar fort, 105
Kanishka (Kushan emperor), 36, 37, 39
Kanjwal, Hafsa, 183
Karan Nagar, 137
*Karkhanas* (workshops), 1, 213
Karkota dynasty, 21–5, 34, 67
Kashani, Abu Talib Kalim, 113, 122, 123
Kashgar, 198
*Kashmir and Kashghar* (Bellew), 134
Kashmir Club, 135
Kashmiri shawl, 81, 97, 119, 136, 144, 224–6
Kashyap Rishi (Hindu sage), 35
*Katha Sarit Sagara*, 48
Khan, Argun, 74
Khan, Asaf, 188
Khan, Ishaq, 155
Khan, Jafar, 199
Khan, Nawab Ali Mardan, 168
Khan, Nawab Danishmand, 105
Khan, Sadar Atta Muhammad, 182
Khan, Saqi Mustad, 109
Khan-i Khanan, Abdul Rahim, 152
Khanqah-i Maula, 73, 74–81, 123, 124, 171, 174, 217
  construction, 78
  disputes about the ownership, 78
  Hamdani's arrival, 76
  Hindus visit, 76
  reconstruction of, 80–1
  structure, 80
*khanqahs* (Sufi hospices), 3, 62, 68
Khilji Sultanate, 44
Khrushchev, Nikita, 193
Khurasan, 122
Khusrau, Amir, 113
*khwajas*, 16–17
Koch, Ebba, 15–16
Koh-i Maran, 85, 86, 94, 108, 114, 160, 182
Kota Rani, 63–4
Kothi Bagh, 192
Kozighar shop, 171
Kozighars, 170–1
Kralwari, Pir Maqbool Shah, 13
Kshemendra, 12
Kumarajiva, monk, 35–6
Kushan Empire, 2, 36–9, 40, 46

Ladakh, 50, 51, 69, 142
Lahore, 9, 80, 113, 120, 151, 183, 224–5
Laila, 166
Lakshmi (goddess), 10
Lalitaditya, Muktapida, 21–4, 25, 26
Libya, 231
Lion Gates (Siṃhadvar), 47, 49
Lion of the Desert (1981) (movie), 231
Lipton tea, 201
Lipton, Thomas, 200

# INDEX

*Maasir-i-Alamgiri*, 109
Madhyantika, monk, 35
Madin Saheb, 208
Maha Kali (goddess), 75, 77
Mahjoor, Abdal, 36
Mahjoor, Pirzada Ghulam Ahmad, 36
"Maikhanah-i Raz", 151
Makhdum, Shaykh Hamza, 183
Malkah, 123–4
Mansur, Ustad, 110, 173
Manucci, Niccolao, 105, 109
maps/map-making, 141–5
   Jaipur Map, 143–5
   Murray map, 143
   trekking, 141–2
Marshall, Sir John, 92
Mashadi, Tughra, 122–3
Mashhad, 208
Masjid-i Dara, 80
Masjid-i Mulla Akhund, 80
Masjid-i Nau, 80
*matha* (Hindu monastery), Dedhmar, 61
Maulana Azad Library, 173
*mazar*, 120–1, 122, 124
Mazar-i Kalan, 44, 124
Mazar-i Salatin, 99–100, 124, 144
Mazar-i Shoura, 119–24
Mehta, Zubin, 189
Meshhad, 224
migration, 67–8, 119–20
Mihirakula, 43–4
Mohra Hydroelectric power plant, 191–2
Mohyi al-Din, Shaykh Ghulam, 221–2

Mongke Khan, 58–9
Mongols, 73
   intrusion into Kashmir, 53, 57–64
   Zilchu, raid of, 57, 58, 59
Montgomerie, Lieutenant, 143
Moorcroft, William, 14–15, 172–3
Morison, Margaret Cotter, 133
Mughals, 2, 105–15
   Bibi's land, 205–8 tea, 197–208
   boats, 106–7
   garden, 28, 110–11, 165–75
   imperial albums (*muraqqa nigari*), 15–16, 48–9, 108
   merchants and Kashmiri shawl, 221–6
   occasions set, 179–84
   poets, 151–6
Mujrim, 222–4
Mukhtar, Umar, 231
Mulla Kabir cemetery, 88
Murray map, 143
*musafir mazar*, 207
Mussolini, Benito, 231

Naagar Nagar, 108, 110, 111, 112, 114, 144, 166–8
Nanking, 36
Naqshbandi, Shah Niyaz, 199
Naseem Bagh, 183
Nau Shahr, 85–8
Nauroz, 180–1
"nautch house", 155
Nayar, Kuldip, 9
Nazaroff, Pavel Stepanovich, 134
Nigeen Lake, 167
*Nilamata Purana*, 35, 46, 51

# INDEX

*nirvana*, 9
Nishat Bagh, 183, 188
Nur Jahan, Empress, 94, 110, 170, 189–90
Nurbakshiyyas, 160
Nursingarh, 137

Oriental Library, 15–16

*Padshahnama*, 107
Pakistan, 192–3
*Palaces, Gardens and the Buildings of the Heart-Pleasing Kashmir* (Badakshi), 112
Pandrethan, 33, 40, 41
Pani Mandir (Water Temple), 40, 41
Parihaspur (modern Devar-Parihaspora), 24–5, 26
  Kani Shahr (The Stone City), 28
Paris, 225
Partition, 2, 10
pashmina trade, 14
*Pashtunwali*, 182
Pattan, 25
Peshawar, 225
Phillimore, RH, 142
Plassey, Battle of (1757), 142
Poland, 230
Poonch, 192
Pravarapur, 27, 33, 85
  Bilhana on, 45–6
  as City of Pravara, 33
  geographical location, 33, 34
  Harsha favoured, 49
  as Hun territory, 44

Kalhana on, 36–7, 45, 47
  named, 42
  palace and gates, 46, 47–8, 49
  roads, 46
  twelve-storey mansions, 45
  Xuanzang on, 34–5, 36
Pravarasena I, 42
Pravarasena II, 42
Punjab, 43, 69, 119–20, 224, 225
Puranadhisthana, 33

Qays, 166
Qizilbash, 167
Qudsi, Hajji Muhammad Jan, 113, 122
Quinn, Anthony, 231
Quran, 16, 108, 123, 206, 208, 218, 231
Qureshi, Mehran, 68

Raghunath Mandir, 127–30, 174
Rahi, Rehman, 233
Rai, Mridu, 78
*Rais-al Tujjar* ( the lord of the merchants), 225–6
*Raisala-i Saifi*, 221
*Rajatarangini* (Kalhana), 22, 35
Ram, Diwan Moti, 128
Ram, Lord, 127
Ramzan, 187, 189, 205, 207
Ratnakantha, 44
*Rayisnama-i Kashmir* (Book of the Wealthy Kashmiris), 208, 223
Razidhaen, 85–7
Reshi, 160
Rinchana, 59–60, 61–2
Rinchanapur, 61–2

255

# INDEX

*Risalah-i Firdausiya*, 122
Roshan Ara Begum, 105–6, 109
Royal Asiatic Society of Great Britain, 151

Saadat, Mufti Muhammad Shah, 119, 120
Saadi, Shaykh, 109
Sabzwari, Mir Husayn, 187, 189
Sadiq, Ghulam Muhammad, 36
Saeeb, Nyami, 9
*Sakinat-ul-Awliya*, 112
Sali Noyan, 59
Santosh, Ghulam Rasul, 80, 141
Saraf Kadal, 136
Saudi Arabia, 68
Schimmel, Annemarie, 189
Seljuks, 93
Seth, Vikram, 172
Shab-i Barat, 189
Shab-i Qadr, 189
Shah Jahan, Emperor, 80, 106–7, 109, 152, 154, 155, 161, 170, 188, 226
    Salim Tehrani at the court of, 121–2
Shah Mir, 62–3, 64
*Shah Nama*, 122
Shah, Khwaja, 199
Shah, Mahdah, 223
Shah, Pir Hasan, 77
Shah, Sikandar, 78, 93
Shah, Taimur, 168
Shahjahanabad (Delhi), 105, 110, 154
Shahmiri Sultanate, 44, 64, 68, 93, 99, 100
Shahr-Ashub (The City's Misfortune, or The City's Disturber), 221
Shalimar Bagh, 155, 183, 187
Shalimar, 152, 170, 187, 192
Shankaravarman, King, 25
Shawl, Khwaja Said al-Din, 226
Shawl, Khwaja Sana-al Lah, 226
Shaykh Bagh, 135, 137
Sherghari (The Citadel of the Lion), 156, 168, 174
Shia, 160
Shihab al-Din, 68–9
Shikoh, Dara, 188
Shirazi, Hafiz, 16, 109, 123, 124, 154, 207
Shirazi, Urfi, 113
Shree Pratap Singh Museum, 41
Shrivara, Pandit, 91–2
Sialkot, 43
Sikandar, Sultan, 64
Sikh rule, 224–5
Silk Road, 23, 39
Simeon Stylites, monk, 52
Simnani, Ala al-Dawla, 74
Singh, Behma, 222
Singh, Maharaja Gulab, 127, 208, 222
Singh, Maharaja Hari, 192
Singh, Maharaja Pratap, 133, 191
Singh, Maharaja Ranbhir, 127, 136, 144–5, 222
Singh, Maharaja Ranjit, 7,8127, 128, 183, 222
Singh, Mihan, 222
Siudmak, John, 47
Somadeva, 48

# INDEX

Sotheby, 208
Soviet Union, 193, 230, 231
Srinagar
   Bibi's land, 205–8
   as a city of towers, 26
   garden, 165–75
   location and landscape, 11
   looting and oppression, 16–17
   medieval times, 12, 16
   merchants and Kashmiri shawl, 221–6
   migration, 67–8
   *mohallas* (neighbourhoods), 10
   municipality, 136–7
   occasions set, 179–84
   as a paradise (*jannat*), 11
   poets, 151–6
   tea, 197–208
Sugandesha Temple, 25
Suhadev, 59
Suhrawardiyya, 159, 160
*Suitable Boy, A* (Seth), 172
Sumtsek Temple, 50–1
Survey of India, 142
*Survey of Kashmir and Jammu*, 142
Suryavati, Queen, 48

Tabrizi, Saib, 152–3
*tajir-al Isfahani*, 208
Takht-i Sulaiman, 120–1, 143
Talas, Battle of, 23–4
*Tantralouk* (Abhinavagupta), 26–7
*tarah*, 151
*Tarikh-i Kashmir*, 74, 76, 77, 190–1
*Tarikh-i Rashidi*, 86
Tashwan, 156

Taxila, 24
Tehran, 224
Tehrani, Salim, 121–2
temple of Meruvardhanaswami, 40
*Throne Carrier of God, The* (Elias), 77
Tibet, 14, 73
Tibetans, 23
Timur, Amir, 76–7, 100
Timurid architecture, 100–1
Toramana (king of the Huns), 43
tourism, 141
TRC (Tourist Reception Centre), 141
trekking, 141
*Tripitaka*, 36
Tsunth Kul (Apple Canal), 108, 135
Tughlaqs, 93
*Tuhfatul Ahbab* (Ahmad Ali), 78
Tujjar, 159
Turbat Khan, Abu, 226
Turbati, Khwaja Abul Hasan, 152
Turk Shahis, 44
Turkey, 68
Turks, 15, 23, 44, 49, 63
   migration, 68
   Zilchu's invasion, 58
*Tuti Nama* (Nakhshabi), 48–9

Urdu Bazaar, 155–6
Utpala dynasty, 25

Verinag, 107
Victoria, Queen, 134, 135, 144, 191
Vikramaditya VI, 45
Vishnu (Hindu god), 24, 25, 127

# INDEX

*Visnudharmottara Purana*, 25
Vyeth Truwah (The Thirteenth of Vyeth), 190

Wahid, Siddiq, 14
*wasta*, 223–4
Wen, Emperor, 36

Xuanzang (or Hsüen-tsang), 34–5, 36, 43
Xuanzong (T'ang emperor of China), 23

Yarkand, 198
Younghusband, Sir Francis Edward, 174

Zadibal, 87, 208
Zain al-Abidin, Sultan, 52, 88, 100, 101, 112, 190
Zaina Kadal, 192, 199
Zainanagari, 86
Zangpo, Rinchen (monk), 50
Zilchu, raid of, 57, 58, 59